WHAT WORKS FOR WOMEN AT WORK

A WORKBOOK

JOAN C. WILLIAMS, RACHEL DEMPSEY, & MARINA MULTHAUP

What Works for Women at Work

A WORKBOOK

NEW YORK UNIVERSITY PRESS *New York*

NEW YORK UNIVERSITY PRESS
New York
www.nyupress.org

References to Internet websites (URLs) were accurate at the time of writing.
Neither the author nor New York University Press is responsible for URLs
that may have expired or changed since the manuscript was prepared.

ISBN: 978-1-4798-7266-4

For Library of Congress Cataloging-in-Publication data, please contact the
Library of Congress.

New York University Press books are printed on acid-free paper, and their
binding materials are chosen for strength and durability. We strive to use
environmentally responsible suppliers and materials to the greatest extent
possible in publishing our books.

Manufactured in the United States of America

10 9 8 7 6 5 4 3 2 1

Also available as an ebook

Joan dedicates this workbook to Sarah Goldhagen,
with thanks for all her help and support.

Contents

Introduction

Four Patterns Working Women Need to Know

Directions for How to Use This Workbook

This workbook was designed to be used in conjunction with *What Works for Women at Work: Four Patterns Working Women Need to Know*. For the women who read *What Works*, this workbook will help you put those ideas into action. It's the owner's manual for your career.

If you are having a specific problem at work, look in the table of contents for the relevant section and work through it. You can first attack what feels most important to you, but working through the workbook section by section will give you the most comprehensive set of tools. Even if a section doesn't seem directly relevant to you, reading through it may help you head off some problems before they trip you up.

And don't forget to have fun!

*   *   *

Here are the four patterns women need to know:

1. **Prove-It-Again!**
2. **The Tightrope**
3. **The Maternal Wall**
4. **The Tug of War**

Prove-It-Again! Bias

Prove-It-Again! bias emerges from the cognitive disconnect between stereotypes of women and stereotypes of business professionals. Jobs like doctor, lawyer, scientist, and businessperson have all traditionally been dominated by men and are often seen to require masculine-typed characteristics like aggression, independence, and analytic ability.[1] This makes it harder for people to picture women succeeding in these roles because women are more likely to be stereotyped as gentle, community oriented, and emotional.[2] As a result, women may have a harder time demonstrating their competence than comparable men do and may be required to give more concrete examples before they're seen as equally capable.

Diagnostic Quiz

Have you encountered Prove-It-Again! problems (check all that apply)?

___*1.* Have you ever realized you make less money than men at your level?

___*2.* Have you ever been told you need more experience for a promotion that was given to a man with the same amount of experience you have?

___*3.* Have people ever kept bringing up a mistake you made as a reason not to promote you, even if it was a one-time slipup that happened a while ago?

___*4.* Have people ever attributed your professional successes to luck?

___*5.* Have you ever been reprimanded for breaking a small rule that men break all the time with no consequences?

___*6.* Have you ever been penalized for failing to meet an objective standard that is rarely or never applied to others?

___*7.* Have you ever been criticized for gossiping, when you were discussing a business problem?

If you checked "yes" for any of these, you've had Prove-It-Again! problems.

Walking the Tightrope

Remember those stereotypes of business professionals—of doctors, programmers, lawyers, and CEOs? Those stereotypes not only are male, but the roles also are seen as requiring masculine-type qualities like ambition, independence, and analytic or technical ability.

So women need to behave in masculine ways in order to be seen as competent, but women are also expected to be feminine—and women who aren't are often seen as unlikable. That's why women often find themselves walking a Tightrope between being seen as too masculine to be likable and too feminine to be competent.

Tightrope problems are divided into problems that stem from the perception that women are "too" feminine, which undermines women's perceived competence, and "too" masculine, which gives rise to criticisms of women's personality: that they have sharp elbows or are outspoken or are prima donnas or not team players.

For example, a study of performance evaluations in tech (a heavily male industry where masculine qualities are seen as important) found that only 59 percent of men's reviews, but 88 percent of women's reviews, contained critical feedback. Even more important, 1 percent of men's reviews contained negative personality criticism, versus an astonishing 66 percent of women's reviews.[3]

Alas, the same woman can run into *both* comments that she is too feminine *and* that she is too masculine. This is particularly true of Asian American women, who find that the space they have to navigate between being seen as too masculine and too feminine is even narrower than for other women. In the highly publicized trial of Ellen Pao, in which she accused her venture capital firm of gender bias against women, the evidence revealed *both* that she had been criticized as too quiet and passive[4] and as too harsh ("not a warm and fuzzy person" and in need of "softening").[5]

Diagnostic Quiz
Have you ever encountered Tightrope problems (check all that apply)?

"Too" Feminine Problems
___*1.* Have people told you that you come across as too quiet or too self-deprecating or that you lack "executive presence"?
___*2.* Have you ever been in a meeting full of men and found it hard to get a word in edgewise or had people talk right over you?
___*3.* Have you ever felt pressure to play a traditionally feminine role—to be the office mom who takes care of everyone else, the dutiful daughter who aligns with a powerful man but never threatens him, or the cheerleader who cheers on the men?
___*4.* Have you ever felt pressure to do the "office housework"—planning parties, taking notes at a meeting, or finding a time everyone can meet, or doing undervalued work while men are given more access to glamour work?

"Too" Masculine Problems
___*1.* Have people told you that you come across as aggressive or demanding or that you have "sharp elbows" or are "not a team player"?
___*2.* Have you ever been criticized for self-promotion in contexts where you were just doing what the men do 24/7, or told you need to "step back to let others shine"?[6]
___*3.* Have you ever gotten angry and been criticized for losing your cool, when the men around you show anger without meeting similar criticism?

If you checked "yes" for any of these, you've had Tightrope problems.

Maternal Wall

You can have Maternal Wall problems whether or not you have children, but these difficulties show up very differently depending on whether or not you are a mom.

Every Day Is Mother's Day (Not)
You leave for maternity a star and return to find you're treated like a drone. Alas, it's all too common. Having children often triggers very strong negative assumptions that women are no longer committed or even competent. One study found that mothers were nearly 80 percent less likely to be hired, only half as likely to be promoted, and offered an average of $11,000 less in salary than *identical* women without children.[7]

Raise Your Hand If You Have No Life

Even if people see you as equally committed as before you had children, they may believe that you should not be. Traditional stereotypes mandate that mothers' first priority should be their children, while fathers' should be to support their families. This means that mothers who work long hours may be seen as bad moms.

What if you don't have children? Too often people then see you as having "no life"—a modern version of the old-fashioned "pathetic spinster" stereotype. Women without children work the longest hours of any group and report the highest levels of workplace harassment,[8] as if not having children means you have no life outside of work.

Diagnostic Quiz

Have you ever encountered Maternal Wall problems (check all that apply)?

Bias Triggered by Motherhood
___*1.* After you became a mother, did you feel you had to prove yourself all over again?
___*2.* Do you have a hard time getting the kind of challenging assignments you got before you had children?
___*3.* Have people criticized you for working hard, saying things like "I don't understand how you can work so hard. My wife could never leave the kids as much as you do"?

Bias against Women without Children
___*4.* Do people assume that you will work holidays or do work no one else wants to do because you have "no life," while parents leave to be with their families?
___*5.* Does your boss consider your request for modified work hours "unreasonable," while parents with young children are given flexible hours?

If you checked "yes" to any of these, you've had Maternal Wall problems.

Tug of War

Sometimes gender bias against women fuels conflict among women. This is often called the "queen bee" syndrome, as if it's an issue of an individual woman with a personality problem. Often, though, women end up pitted against each other because of strategic decisions that ambitious women make to get ahead in an environment shaped by gender bias.

Diagnostic Quiz

Have you ever encountered Tug of War problems (check all that apply)?
___*1.* Do women in your workplace undercut each other in order to secure the one "woman's spot" on a desirable team or committee?

___*2.* Do women hold other women to higher standards than they do men, on the grounds that "that's what it takes to succeed here as a woman"?

___*3.* Is it harder for women professionals to get support from admins, as compared with male professionals? (In environments where most people at the top are men, admins may feel it's a safer bet to align with someone more likely to make it to the top—a man.)

___*4.* Do women criticize each other for being too feminine ("No wonder she never gets promoted wearing clothes like that") or too masculine ("No wonder no one likes her. She's a royal bitch.")?

___*5.* Do women criticize each other over the "right" way to be a mother ("No wonder she hasn't been promoted, given her part-time schedule" or "She just turned into a man. I want to raise my own children, not have a nanny do it.")?

If you checked any of these, you're smack dab in the middle of a Tug of War among women.

Often women support each other, but sometimes gender bias against women fuels conflicts among women. The Tug of War among women reflects several different dynamics. If women feel there's only room for one woman in prized positions, they may try to undercut each other to be that one woman. Women who have experienced discrimination early in their careers often distance themselves from other women because doing so makes sense politically—we call this *strategic distancing*.

The other three patterns of gender bias also can be passed through from woman to woman. Women may hold each other to higher standards because "that's what it takes to succeed here as a woman"—a pass-through of Prove-It-Again! bias. Tightrope bias can also be passed through: "The older women here aren't role models; they just turned into men" (she's too masculine) or "No wonder no one takes her seriously with that little girl voice" (she's too feminine). Maternal Wall is passed through when older women belittle younger women's desire to take a longer parental leave or go part-time: "I worked full time my whole career and *my* kids are fine" (she's a bad worker)—to which younger women often respond, "I want to raise my own kids, not just leave them with a stranger" (she's a bad mother).

It's important to remember that all these kinds of conflict reflect gender bias in the environment, not proof that one woman is a "queen bee." These skirmishes typically stem not from the personality problem of an individual woman but from strategic behavior in the environment that are deeply etched by bias.

I Haven't Met Any of That!

We are extremely pleased to hear that. But not surprised.

Each of these patterns represents a *tendency*: men as a group *tend* to be judged on their potential; women as a group *tend* to be judged on their performance. No pattern describes the experience of all women. In *What Works for Women at Work*, we found that 96 percent of working women had encountered at least *one* of the four patterns, but only 11 percent had encountered *all* of them.[9]

In some workplaces, none of the patterns is a factor. If that's the case where you work, count yourself lucky. You may want to keep reading, because many of the exercises in this workbook are useful even if there's no bias in your current workplace.

It's also sometimes the case that women who don't encounter bias when they are young do encounter it when they are older. Forewarned is forearmed.

Gender Judo

Gender judo is a metastrategy that could come in handy when dealing with lots of different instances of bias. We're introducing it here because we'll be offering ways to apply gender judo throughout the workbook.

The martial art of judo teaches how to use your opponents' momentum to overthrow them. Gender judo uses stereotypes that traditionally have held women back to your advantage. This strategy is not for everyone, as it involves strategically incorporating different traits into your personality at work. We recommend reading over the section and deciding for yourself whether to try it or forget it.

The Basics

The prescriptive stereotype—our cultural understanding of what it means to be a good woman—is someone who is modest, self-effacing, and nice. Our stereotype of a "man to be reckoned with" is very different: someone who is direct, competitive, and ambitious. Guess which tends to be rewarded in the workplace? You got it: those who are direct, competitive, ambitious—and male. If a woman behaves that way, she risks being seen as arrogant or a bitch. That's the Tightrope: women walk a tightrope between being seen as a go-getter *or* as a good person.

Because women risk being dinged both for being too feminine and for being too masculine, the solution is to mix the masculine and the feminine. That's the essence of gender judo: doing a masculine thing in a feminine way in order to avoid backlash. One tech executive described her strategy as "Be warm Ms. Mother 95 percent of the time, so that, when you need to be tough, you can be."[10] Notice how she used a feminine stereotype that typically holds women back—the office mom—but used it strategically to propel herself forward. That's gender judo.

Hillary Clinton used gender judo during the first presidential debate of the 2016 campaign. Clinton, who for most of her career has been dinged for appearing "too masculine" (read: being ambitious, wearing a pant suit, and not confining herself to a winning smile), found a way to "play the woman card," softening her attacks on Donald Trump with a big smile and a few shakes of her shoulders, quickly dubbed "the shimmy" by pundits. Only then did she launch into a point about NATO. We don't think it's a coincidence that her poll numbers went up after that first debate but that she didn't do so well in the second and third debates when she dispensed with the gender judo and came at Trump directly and aggressively. Clinton still "won" the later debates but by an increasingly smaller margin.[11] May the shimmy go down in history as "the best political instinct Clinton has ever acted on" (as one Twitter user called it).[12] We may wish we didn't have to add a shimmy of femininity, but gender judo works.

Should women have to do this? Of course not. But that's a different book: not *What Works for Women at Work* but "What *Should* Work for Women at Work." What *should* work for women—to just be ourselves and be recognized and rewarded as such—ain't happening in many workplaces today. Our goal is to equip you with as many strategies as possible and leave it up to you to decide which ones you want to try and which ones you want to ignore.

How You Come Across

First, let's see what kind of stereotypes you are likely to trigger in people who hold old-fashioned views (and even some young people too).

A self-assessment: put an "X" next to any trait you see in yourself.

_____Aggressive	_____Affectionate
_____Ambitious	_____Cheerful
_____Competitive	_____Compassionate
_____Forceful	_____Gentle
_____A leader	_____Gullible
_____Independent	_____Shy
_____Individualistic	_____Soft-spoken
_____Decisive	_____Sympathetic
_____Self-sufficient	_____Tender
_____Willing to take risks	_____Understanding[13]

Did you check more boxes in the left-hand column or the right-hand column? If you checked more boxes in the right-hand column, you've described yourself as exhibiting predominantly feminine traits. If you checked more boxes in the left-hand column, you've described yourself as having more masculine traits.

Everyone, of course, has a mix of both. Masculine traits are not the opposite of feminine traits. Both sets entail important ways of being human.

In the workplace, however, women who behave in ways traditionally seen as feminine often are seen as less forceful and perhaps less competent, because many high-status jobs are traditionally defined as requiring masculine traits: being analytical, decisive, and willing to take risks. Yet when women display those masculine traits, they may be disliked or seen as lacking in social skills or polish: inadequately sympathetic, friendly, and understanding.

Playing Both Sides

Can you think of a time when you believe your career suffered because you were seen as "too feminine"? Write down a couple of examples if they come to mind:

_____

_____

_____

_____

_____

_____

If you think your career has been hurt, look over the masculine traits listed above and see if there are any that you would feel comfortable infusing into your workplace demeanor. For example, if you notice you don't get the biggest clients because you're more soft-spoken, consider adding some more authority to how you speak. This is gender judo. You don't have to suddenly start yelling everything and change who you are. But blending some masculine traits into your existing skill set could help you get the respect and recognition you deserve.

If this seems interesting or helpful to you, write down three masculine traits you could see yourself trying out:

1. _____

2. _____

3. _____

Next, look back to the times when you feel you've been dinged because you were seen as too feminine. How can you incorporate one of these masculine qualities in a way that still feels authentic? Write down a couple ideas:

_____

_____

_____

_____

_____

_____

_____

Now, pick one and try it out at work. How did it feel?

_____

_____

_____

_____

_____

If you checked more boxes on the left-hand side, then you display more traditionally masculine traits. Use the same exercise to practice gender judo: can you think of a time at work when you nailed it substantively but felt you were dinged because you weren't seen as "approachable" or "warm"?

_____

_____

_____

_____

_____

How could you incorporate some traits that are traditionally associated with femininity to your advantage? For example, you can volunteer to organize an aspect of the company day out or help organize an office party. This type of "office housework" won't rocket you to the top of your company, and you certainly don't want to get stuck doing it all the time (see chapter 13 in the workbook and pages 110–116 in *What Works* for more on this), but this use of gender judo could help you if you're experiencing gender bias for being "too ambitious." List a few ways you could incorporate more femme traits:

_____

_____

_____

_____

_____

_____

Review what you wrote. Could you actually do this in your workplace? Or would it cost you too much political capital?

_____

_____

_____

_____

_____

_____

Hate It? Forget It?

Gender judo is a technique that some women have found helps them deflect bias and more easily advance up the male-dominated corporate ladder. However, as you see, it involves adapting your personality to fit this biased world we live in. Gender judo isn't a way to fix masculine culture; it's a way of allowing you to swim more easily through the salt water.

If gender judo feels too icky to you, don't do it. It turns some people off—particularly women who feel comfortable with traits our culture associates with masculinity and who have been told all their lives not to be so "harsh" (be soft and yielding like a good woman), "tactless" (don't be direct; be soft and tactful), or "abrasive" (for doing something that would be admirably assertive in a man). If this describes you, then hearing _feminists_ appear to say the same thing may be irritating in the extreme.

Moreover, if you are butch or queer, this advice may sound positively soul destroying. No job is worth this.

For most women, however, the reality is that they have a mix of masculine and feminine qualities. To a gender theorist (Joan), this makes sense, because qualities that have been lumped into two apparently dichotomous categories are, in fact, not dichotomous at all. They are different ways of being humans, and most humans draw on both columns.

Probably, if you're a working woman, you already use gender judo, maybe even without realizing it. You may speak differently at work than you do with your family. You may dress differently at work than you do on your days off. You may show your emotions differently at work than you do with your partner or with your friends. Recently Joan gave a speech in which she described gender judo. A woman law firm partner came up to her afterward and said, "You know, you really made me think. I just got awarded one of the highest bonuses in the firm, and today I wore this hot-pink top—as if to say, 'I may be one of the highest paid people here, but I'm still a woman.' I see now I was doing gender judo without knowing it."

What's an unfortunate reality in our society is that gender roles encourage us to limit ourselves to one arbitrary set of qualities that may not be the best fit for our personalities or for the roles we need to play at work. Too often, women have to make the choice between being liked but not respected or being respected but not liked.[14] Gender judo is a tool that you can use to try and navigate the no-win situation that women sometimes find ourselves in by adapting the traits you show to fit your environment. If you can use gender judo to help your situation, while still feeling true to yourself, then go for it. But (again) no job is worth feeling inauthentic for. If using gender judo feels like a stretch you're willing to try, try it. If it feels more like a lie that you're unwilling to live, then don't go there.

About the Workbook (from Joan)

We were all taken by surprise by the success of *What Works for Women at Work*. There's a hunger for advice that combines research with wisdom.

We have the research, and I interviewed the savviest women I knew—they contributed the wisdom. The hunger for concrete advice that's not just free association keeps fueling the book.

That's why Lean In kindly invited me to do videos based on the book that, at last count, had nearly half a million views. (Available in Virgin Air flights as free content and at http://leanin.org/education/introduction-to-what-works-for-women-at-work/). We are grateful for Lean In's support and give thanks to Sheryl Sandberg and Rachel Thomas.

This workbook takes things a step further. It helps you really digest the advice offered in *What Works for Women at Work* through exercises that apply the advice to your own life, step by step in a systematic way.

A central premise of *What Works for Women at Work* is that this kind of advice only works as a cross-generational conversation. My daughter, Rachel Dempsey, who co-wrote the original book, has long since moved on. She undertook the project because she had decided to be a writer rather than a lawyer, and she's now . . . a lawyer—but also a writer. My new coauthor, Marina Multhaup, fills Rachel's very big shoes. Marina has kept me grounded in the experience of younger women; together, we speak to the experience of a very broad range of women.

We've also included new material in this workbook, which reflects the leadership programming at the Center for WorkLife Law, where both Marina and I work. This advice ranges from insights into how to be effective in meetings to how to live life as a happy person. We urge you to take a look.

I've spent a lifetime developing these exercises. They are what I've learned to do over the course of a 40-year career. I suspect they'll prove useful for you, too.

PART I

Get Over Yourself

You've learned about the four patterns of bias that—alas—affect many women on a daily basis. These patterns describe the bias that comes from outside of women, and you'll learn creative solutions for combating these patterns.

But bias also comes from within women ourselves.

Diagnostic Quiz

(Check all that apply)

___*1.* Do you tend to present your ideas tentatively, using phrases like "Don't you think . . . ," "I wonder if . . . ," or "I may be wrong but . . . ," rather than simply stating what you think?

___*2.* Do you tend to accept blame when something's not your fault?

___*3.* Do you take on tasks like organizing the office holiday party because, well, you just like doing it?

___*4.* Do you, more than others on your team, volunteer to do the less glorious work in order to prove your value?

___*5.* Do you have different expectations of male than female bosses, notably by expecting the women to always be supportive?

___*6.* Do you criticize other women on the grounds that they are bitches or that they have "just turned into men"?

___*7.* Do you criticize other women on the grounds that they are pushovers or just suck up to the men or lack executive presence?

If you checked any of these, you need to ask yourself whether you yourself are participating in gender bias. You may not be. Chapters 1 through 4 will help you decide.

1

Overcoming Your Own Prove-It-Again! Bias

Stop Apologizing

📖 (Read with *What Works* pages 117–120)

Who wants to be the kind of jerk who refuses to apologize when she does something wrong?

That's not the kind of apologizing we're talking about here. Write down an example of a time when you apologized because you'd really messed up.

_____

_____

_____

_____

_____

_____

Now write down a time when you apologized just to make sure no one saw you as arrogant or as a general social lubricant, even though you had done nothing wrong, and no one had even hinted that. For example, in a context where someone else made a mistake or where it's unclear who did so, you may have said, "I'm so sorry. I should have made it clear what time zone this was in."

_____

_____

_____

_____

_____

Can you see the difference? When you've done something wrong, apologizing is a signal of strength. It's a signal that you have the self-knowledge to recognize that you've messed up, the maturity to own up to your mistake, and the confidence not to let one mistake undermine your sense that your contributions going forward still have value.

But if you keep apologizing as a general social lubricant, then people see you as someone who is worried, worried, worried that she does not bring value to the table. If you don't believe in yourself, why should others believe in you?

Now go back to the time when you apologized even though you had done nothing wrong. How could you have handled the situation differently? First, identify the goal you were seeking to achieve by framing your contribution as an apology.

Some common reasons:

"I just didn't want to come off as arrogant." In other words, you were worried about backlash for not being sufficiently modest, self-effacing, and nice. Try this: the next time you're tempted to apologize, just state your views in a direct way, with quiet confidence. What happened?

If you got pushback that sent the message that you are not allowed to present your views that way, then the bias is outside your head, not inside your head.

"I just thought I was being polite. But the other person *so* didn't get it." Research by sociolinguist Deborah Tannen shows that men and women tend to have quite different conversational patterns. Women's default mode typically is "sharing troubles": "listen to the bad thing I did." "No, no, *I* did something much worse." "Let me tell you about the time . . ." This ritualized form of self-abasement is a common way women bond.[1]

Men, not so much. Men's default mode is a friendly one-upmanship where the goal is to avoid being in a one-down position. So when women come in offering self-deprecation, men sometimes just don't get it. "What kind of a loser is she," they ask themselves, "to be handing me the one-up position without competing for it?"

Maybe men's default mode bugs you so much that you want to work in an environment where it's not a factor. If that's the way you feel, go for it. But that rules out a lot of jobs—many of them really good, desirable ones. So you may need to widen your repertoire to include men's default mode as well as women's.

"I had gotten feedback that I come on too strong, so I figured I had nothing to lose by softening it up a bit." If you know that you command authority and are using apologies as a softener to avoid backlash—and it's working—then keep on doing it. That's gender judo.

Learn to Accept a Compliment

📖 (Read with *What Works*, "Strategy 2: Get Over Yourself," on pages 46–49)

As women, we learn from a young age to deflect compliments. So think of a recent compliment and write it down.

_____

_____

What did you say in response (e.g., "I got lucky" or "It was really a team effort")?

_____

_____

If you accepted it, congratulations! Way to own your success. If not, come up with three things you could have said to graciously accept the compliment and acknowledge your hard work (e.g., "Thanks. I worked really hard, so it's great to see it paying off" or "Thanks. You've made my day"). Again, if you don't value your contributions, others won't either.

1. _____

2. _____

3. _____

The next time someone gives you a compliment, don't deflect it—accept it. Pushing praise aside can make it feel awkward to give you a compliment. Accepting it signals that you know your own worth and makes others acknowledge it as well.

Be Willing to Ask for a Promotion

Studies show that if there are nine requirements for promotion, women tend to wait until they have all nine.[2] Men will ask for promotion much earlier: they are under gender pressures to prove they are "ambitious," which is seen as a desirable trait in men (but sometimes suspect in women, alas!). This is a natural response by women to the unspoken reality that they may have to be twice as good to get half as far.

If the men are going for it, you need to, too. If you wait to be perfect, you're going to be waiting forever, and in the meantime, you'll be lagging behind others who are less qualified but more confident.

Consider the job you'd like to be promoted to. What are the requirements?

_____

_____

_____

_____

_____

Which of these requirements do you have now?

_____

_____

_____

_____

_____

Which don't you have?

_____

_____

_____

_____

_____

Now approach someone in your network at work—someone a little more senior would be perfect. Ask them whether it's time for you to apply for that promotion. If they say no, ask what skills or experiences you need in order to get ready for the promotion. (If you have a question in your mind about whether you've asked the right person, ask someone else—but not more than three people. You can't spend all of your political capital on any one thing.) Write down the results here:

_____

_____

_____

_____

_____

Now go to your supervisor, and tell them that you are interested in being promoted and that you believe that you need the following skills in order to be ready. Ask whether they can give you opportunities to develop those skills, stressing that you want to be a team player but believe that developing additional skills will make you more valuable to the company. Report on the results of that conversation here:

_____

_____

_____

_____

_____

What if your supervisor indicates that they don't think you are ready for the kinds of stretch assignments you have indicated you want? Then ask your supervisor what you need to do to get ready for the next step and check back in when you've gotten there. If you never seem to get there, then go to part 7, "Leave or Stay?," to assess whether it's time for you to think about finding a new job.

Do Something before You're Ready

📖 (Read with *What Works*, "Strategy 2: Get over Yourself," on pages 46–49)

More generally, it's a good muscle to flex: do something before you're ready. It doesn't even have to be work related. It can be that maybe you've been meaning to apply for a promotion or considered throwing your hat in the ring for a competitive project, but it can also be something like skydiving or going to an upper-level yoga class even though you still haven't mastered the standing splits. Before you do it, answer the following questions.

What are you afraid of?

_____

_____

_____

_____

_____

What do you imagine happening if you try?

_____

_____

_____

_____

Consider the worst-case scenario. How bad is it? What would you do if it happened?

_____

_____

_____

_____

Not that bad, is it? So now go do it. Whatever it is, congratulations. How do you feel when it's over? Did the worst happen? If not, how do you feel? If so, was the worst as bad as you thought it was?

_____

_____

_____

_____

Chances are you were successful at whatever you tried, and even if you weren't, you got something out of it and gained some new skills.

Go to part 4, "Navigating Workplace Politics," for more strategies to address Prove-It-Again! bias.

2

Overcoming Your Own Tightrope Bias

Project Credibility and Confidence

📖 (Read with *What Works*, pages 85–87)

Search the Internet for six images: three where people are holding their bodies in a feminine way and three where people project a masculine posture.

In which set do the people in question seem "centered"—have their weight evenly distributed between their feet? In which set do the people seem less commanding or off-balance?

_____

In which set do the people in question take up a lot of space? In which set do the people have their arms or legs folded in and otherwise not take up much space?

_____

_____

_____

_____

In all primates, standing with weight centered signals high status and dominance; standing off-center signals subordination. In all primates, taking up space signals dominance, while taking up little space signals deference. These principles hold if you are sitting down in a meeting. Sitting with your weight centered and taking up space signal high status.

When you are in a meeting, do you tend to signal status or subordination?

_____

_____

_____

_____

Psychological research shows that standing like Wonder Women for two to three seconds—feet firmly planted, taking up space—can *literally make you be more self-confident*.[1] For more on this subject, check out Amy Cuddy's fabulous Ted Talk.[2]

And then there's your voice. People tend to decide where to pitch their voices in high school, and women often decide to pitch their voices high and make them breathy (as opposed to resonant) in order to be heard as feminine. Some people make this voice work well for them: an example is the prolific actress Jennifer Tilly.[3] But in many traditionally male careers, a high-pitched "air voice" will not command authority.

In business contexts—in a meeting, on the phone, or when giving a presentation—how do you pitch your voice?

Do you think that this way of pitching your voice works well for you? If it does, don't do a thing. Count yourself lucky!

If you think that your voice is undercutting your ability to project credibility and confidence, work with a friend (or just a voice-memo app on your phone) and describe the first job you ever had for two minutes. First, use a traditionally feminine tone with a breathy vocal quality. Then, redo your two-minute spiel with a traditionally masculine tone and more resonant vocal quality. Do this two or three times a week for four weeks, until you feel that you can switch back and forth at will between the two different styles.

Do a similar exercise with your posture. Practice with a friend (or just in front of a mirror) and describe the plot of your favorite movie for two minutes. Notice how you are naturally inclined to distribute your weight (e.g., do you shift from side to side, cross your legs, put more weight on one side?). Repeat your favorite movie plot, this time standing with your weight evenly centered on both legs, feet firmly planted. Do this exercise a couple of times a week, until you are able to feel the difference between the two without thinking about it. This will make it easier for you to assume the "power stance" when you need to and turn it off when you don't.

Are there some situations—for example, when you are presenting a threat to someone—when you would want to present a more submissive tone and posture? Give an example from your own workplace.

_____

_____

_____

_____

_____

Are there other situations when you would want to present a more confident and commanding tone and posture? Give examples.

_____

_____

_____

_____

_____

For more on this, see Deborah Gruenfeld's work on "playing high" and "playing low."[4] Being able to do both are tools every woman should have in her toolbox.

Stop Volunteering for Office Housework / Getting Over Your Inner Handmaiden

📖 (Read with *What Works*, pages 65–68)

"But I Like to Plan Parties!"

Okay, we get that. Some people do. But you should know that party planning typically is not the most strategic way to spend your time at work. Do you like party planning so much that you are willing to *both* do the party planning *and* also do the assignments that are more work relevant and more highly valued? That means you will be working longer hours than people who dispense with party planning. Are you okay with that?

Our advice: if you love party planning, do it once, do it well, and move on. When people say, "But you are so good at it," respond, "The same skills that make me a good party planner also mean I'd be good at . . . ," then name the career-enhancing assignment you want. And suggest someone else for party planning.

If you're having trouble, here's a matrix to help you think this through:

Housework	Pros	Cons
Planning parties	Builds community. You may be seen as a good team player.	Takes time away from "real" work. You may be perceived as too busy for more career-enhancing assignments. You may be seen as someone who does not understand how to prioritize so that you get "good" work.
Taking notes	You can use note taking as a way of snagging good follow-up assignments for yourself. You can use note taking as a way to shaping the agenda going forward: what gets written down is often what gets remembered.	Taking notes makes it harder for you to participate fully in the meeting. Taking notes depicts you as a facilitator of other people's thought rather than a thought leader.
Getting people on the conference call, ordering the lunch	Meetings can't happen unless people get on the line and don't have to starve! Having everyone attend to these tasks has a leveling effect on the company.	Again, attending to these tasks often impedes your ability to participate fully in the meeting. If these tasks are done chiefly by women, then they may undercut women's perceived leadership potential.

"I Feel Comfortable Doing What I'm Doing. Everyone Praises Me to the Skies. Why Should I Change What I'm Doing?"

This a common situation. Here's the unpleasant fact: just because everyone praises you to the skies for doing undervalued work doesn't mean that they will promote you for doing it. Chapter 13 will help you identify what's valued in your environment and what's office housework. Once you've done that, decide whether you really want to be promoted. If you genuinely don't care, then keep on doin' the housework—enjoy. Just don't kid yourself about your long-term career prospects.

"But I Love Mentoring—and I Think It's Important to Help Advance Other Women"

First of all, thank you—we mean that. Women definitely wouldn't be getting ahead at the same rate without you.

That said, if women continue to do all the mentoring, running the summer program, and planning the off-sites, these important team-building functions will continue to be undervalued, and men will have more time than women to spend on career-enhancing assignments. And you are modeling to other women that it's appropriate to ask women to do tasks that, while important, are undervalued. So choose one function that's not overly time-consuming that you really feel is important and decide how much time you can dedicate to it on top of your other work—without overworking. Then let the other opportunities go. If you want to do another team-building function, then, fine, do that one next year.

How much time do you spend doing mentoring, running the summer program, planning off-sites, or in other team-building functions?

_____

_____

_____

_____

_____

_____

What's the one you like best?

_____

Now develop a succession plan for how to transition the others to someone else. Note that if you are deep into this hole, your succession plan may take some time to achieve. Here's an example: "Jim, I have really enjoyed the paperclips committee for the last six years. But next year, I really want to transition to the X or Y committee. I think Keith would be great for paperclips: it would help him get to know more about our supply chain and would introduce him to Donna, an important internal contact at this point in his career. Would you like me to start training him so he can take over paperclips? I will talk to [the relevant person] about my interest in X committee. Would you do that, too? What do I need to get ready to take on that successfully?"

Describe your succession plan here.

_____

_____

_____

_____

_____

_____

See chapter 13 in the workbook for additional strategies for getting housework off your plate or making it work for you. Also, see pages 113–117 in *What Works* for more.

"I Want Everyone to Like Me!"

"With being thought of as a bitch . . . I kind of aspire to that a little bit because . . . actually it's a very effective perception to have," one professor told us.[5] If it works, it works! Go for it. But what if you're the kind of gal who just wants everyone to like you?

Having people like you is a good career move . . . up to a point. But remember, work is not a popularity contest. People have not only to like you; they have to respect your work. Otherwise, you're a nice person who's dispensable when the going gets competitive. "As you evolve in your career, you realize that you're just not going to be friends with everyone and that's okay. It doesn't mean that you can't work well with them. I am the prototype of the 'girl who wants to be liked.' And so my personal challenge is it makes me uncomfortable even to acknowledge that."[6] Remember this is work, not high school.

If your first priority is for everyone to like you, you won't be willing to put your foot down when you need to, and you risk people walking all over you. Sound familiar? If so, give an example of a time when you sacrificed making a hard business decision because you were afraid that people wouldn't like you for it.

_____

_____

_____

_____

_____

_____

Let's take a step back. Explain how you bring value at work.

_____

_____

_____

_____

_____

_____

Now describe a situation in which it was impossible for you to show how you bring value, because someone was voicing over you or steamrolling you.

_____

_____

_____

_____

_____

_____

If you can't show how you bring value, no one's going to know about the value you bring. So you need to learn how to put your foot down. How could you have asserted yourself in a way that kept the fences mended to the maximum extent possible but also got the job done?

_____

_____

_____

_____

_____

Here's the basic principle: if you have to choose between being nice and being competent, choose competent. Remember, better to be a bitch than a doormat.

Also remember that there's an important difference between doormat nice and being polite, respectful, considerate, and compassionate.

What if there's no way on God's green earth that you can put your foot down at work without totally alienating people who are walking all over you? Go directly to part 7, "Leave or Stay?" *It may be time to think about finding a new job.*

"It's My Party, I Can Cry If I Want To"

(Read with "Cry Me A River," on page 119 of *What Works*)

If it *is* your party, cry if you want to. But if you're at work with men, remember that having a woman cry makes most men uncomfortable. Strong taboos discourage men from crying, with the message that crying is a signal of weakness.

If you're crying a lot at work, you probably need a new job. What if you cry a little or if you're just terrified that you might cry and ruin everything?

Relax, you probably won't cry. If you feel like it and sense that crying's not the best solution, try these:

1. **Leave the office and take the rest of the day off, if that will slip under the radar screen. No job's worth that kind of nonsense, and you will return to work tomorrow** in a far better frame of mind. Make sure you reach out to your network to help you talk things through.

2. If you can't leave, shut your office door, have a good cry, get ahold of yourself, and do low-key stuff for the rest of the day.

3. If leaving's not an option and you don't have a private office, go to the ladies' room, get ahold of yourself, and then come back to a low-key rest of the day in which you put off talking with people if possible. Just be really, really busy and set a time to talk tomorrow.

If you do cry in a work situation, remember that you need to overcome the impression that you're out of control and that crying's a sign of weakness. Here's one formula: One New Girl told us that her physical response to anger is to cry. She tells people, "When I'm crying, it's because I'm pissed. This is what it looks like when I'm mad."[7] Notice how she converted what may otherwise be interpreted as a sign of weakness into a sign of strength.

Sheryl Sandberg, the chief operating officer at Facebook, acknowledged crying at work: "I've cried at work. I've told people I've cried at work."[8] If you're as powerful as Sandberg, you can afford to give away a little of your power. Just make sure you have some to give away first.[9]

3

Overcoming Your Own Maternal Wall Bias

"I feel like I'm not doing a good job either at home or at work." Why do working moms so often feel like utter failures?

Take a minute to jot down what it takes to be an ideal worker.

1. _____

2. _____

3. _____

4. _____

5. _____

Now take a minute to jot down what it takes to be an ideal mother.

1. _____

2. _____

3. _____

4. _____

5. _____

If you're like most people, your answers probably reflected that the ideal worker is always available for work, while the ideal mother is always available to her children.

News flash: this is impossible.

That means that all women with both children and a job feel like they are not living up to their own ideals. That's not because they are inadequate. It's because societal ideals, of the ideal worker and the ideal mother, just don't fit. They're inconsistent. So it's that simple. That's why working moms so often feel they're not doing anything up to their standards.

Getting Over the Ideal Worker in Your Head

Let's examine both those ideals. First, the ideal worker. Defining the ideal worker as someone always available to his employer made sense in the 1960s, when the professional workforce was composed largely of men married to homemakers. It makes no sense today, when over 60 percent of children live in households in which all parents are employed.[1]

Sure, it's inconvenient when someone goes on maternity leave. But it's also inconvenient when a man has a heart attack or prostate cancer. When a man has a heart attack, people cover without comment, except to express concern for their colleague's health. When a woman has a baby, though—OMG, it's an imposition on everyone. Why?

Employers accept the fact that when men have prostate cancer, that's just a cost of hiring a workforce, but when a woman has a baby, that's seen as an extra, avoidable cost. Why? Because they still, unconsciously, define the ideal worker as a man. So costs uniquely associated with men are seen as costs of hiring a workforce, while costs uniquely associated with women are seen as unbearable impositions—on their employer and on their co-workers.

This is pretty silly. In this day and age, the costs and inconvenience associated with workers having children are costs of hiring a workforce. Robots would be better, for sure: they have neither babies nor bodies. But until employers can hire robots and be done with it, they need to change their attitude about workers who have children. You need to, too. You should not be apologetic or guilty that you cannot live up to a societal ideal that is fundamentally screwed up.

Give five reasons why it doesn't make sense to define the ideal worker as someone who is always available to their employer.

1. _____

2. _____

3. _____

4. _____

5. _____

Decades of studies have documented that family-friendly workplaces save employers money in all kinds of ways. They decrease turnover and absenteeism.[2] They allow employers to tap the full workforce, rather than limiting them to men married to homemakers and people without children. Increasingly, employers risk losing fathers as well as mothers if they insist on the old-fashioned definition of the ideal worker: more and more men see being a good father as someone who is involved with the daily care of his children. These men will leave workplaces where they are expected to be available for endless work.

In addition, burnt-out employees are less productive and less innovative.[3] Is there anyone who will seriously argue that someone working an 80-hour week is as efficient as someone who is leading a balanced, well-rested life?

It's time to get over the Ideal Worker in Your Head. That ideal is unrealistic. It's not good for workers. And it's not good for employers. The real ideal is someone who leads a balanced life, who comes to work fresh and motivated, gives their best, and then goes home. Of course, sometimes professionals have to work long hours. But to insist—to yourself—that you live up to the ideal of the Man Who Mistook His Job for a Life[4] is not workable. Just get over it.

Name five reasons why it is in your employer's self-interest to redefine the ideal worker as someone who has important commitments outside of work.

1. _____

_____

_____

2. _____

_____

_____

3. _____

_____

_____

4. _____

_____

_____

5. _____

_____

_____

Getting Over the Ideal Mother in Your Head

The good mother is seen as someone who is "always available to her children," according to one study.[5] Do you believe that?

If so, you're in for a lot of guilt. If you want to stay home full-time, God bless, and stop reading. But if you don't, read on.

Think of five reasons why it might not be best for your kids if you stay home full-time and list them below. It may help to read Joan's first:

1. *Life is unpredictable.* You never know when, God forbid, your husband may become incapacitated or otherwise unavailable. And the children of divorced parents are less likely to reach the educational level or class status of their fathers—because their mothers are often left economically vulnerable.[6]

2. *Don't worry, be happy.* Studies show that what matters is not whether you stay home or go to work but whether you're happy with the choices you make.[7] This

makes sense. After all, as we've seen, no choice is a piece of cake. But your mood has a profound effect on your children.[8] Are you modeling angst at your inability to be both the perfect mother and the ideal worker? Do you carry a profound sense of loss because you gave up your career? That's not the way you want your kids to remember their childhood.

3. *Helicopter parenting is not good for kids.* If your ideal is to discover every little microtalent your kids have and develop it *immediately*, you're motivated by love but may also be communicating anxiety. "How can I make sure my son gets into Harvard?" asked one mom at a Washington, D.C., preschool meeting. Helicopter parenting is an expression of economic anxiety.[9] You don't want your kids to get the message that you will think they are failures unless they get into Harvard. You want your kids to get the message that you will think they are failures if they aren't good people: kind, caring, conscientious. And as study after study shows, there are many paths to the top in the U.S. We are not in France, where if you don't get into Sciences Po, you will never be a diplomat. So try this out for size: raise your kids with a quiet sense that everything will turn out just fine. Then they will internalize a quiet sense of peace. Your choice: inner peace or anxiety.

4. *Your career can help your children as they grow older.* Read part 3, "Networks." Fifty to 70 percent of professionals get jobs through social networks.[10] Both Rachel and my son, Nick, got their first professional jobs through my network of contacts. Children do not stay babies forever; once they've grown, you can help them more and relate to them in a wider range of ways if you've maintained your career.

5. *Be able to pay your own bills.* Being economically dependent often profoundly affects the power dynamic in a relationship, sociologists have found over and over again since the 1960s. (Robert Blood and Donald Wolfe initiated this line of research.)[11]

Now it's your turn:

1. _____

_____

2. _____

_____

3. _____

_____

4. _____

_____

5. _____

_____

Please don't repeat these arguments to your friends who are stay-at-home mothers. (If you are tempted, see chapters 4 and 15 in the workbook on the Tug of War among women.) Remember that they made the best choice they could, just as you did: in a society that defines the ideal worker and the ideal parent in inconsistent ways, all of the available choices are flawed. Our goal here is to bolster your decision to remain in the workforce, so you can do precisely what the stay-at-home moms are doing: modeling for their kids how to make hard choices and be at peace with them.

Now let's get rid of those voices in your head that are keeping you up at night. Take the time right now to name five ways that the fact that you're working enhances your children's lives.

1. _____

_____

2. _____

_____

3. _____

_____

4. _____

_____

5. _____

_____

Here are some that Joan came up with:

1. My amazing nannies gave my children amazing gifts I could never give them. They gave Rachel a sense of fun, fashion, and whimsy. They gave both Nick and Rachel a sense of peace, centeredness, and family—not to mention a command of Spanish. After all, children traditionally have been raised by groups of adults. The idea that it's ideal for one isolated woman to be the sole-source provider for her children is not convincing. As perfect as you are, other trusted adults can give your kids things that you can't give them.

2. When the children were little, I could get some time to myself. That was important because being in charge of two small kids is really hard! Working renewed my energy and equilibrium.

3. I really love my work and would have been bereft to give it up.

4. I am an anxious person. Having both work and family allowed me to keep my perspective on both.

5. Now that both children have grown, the contacts I've made through my career have enabled me to help both of my kids in their careers at crucial points.

What if your kids are in day care?

Raising children takes a village. Without the help of teachers, nannies, tutors, aunts and uncles, grandparents, and friends, your kids wouldn't learn as much—and you would never get a break! So if you can afford it, day care can be a great option to allow your children to learn from other people (plus you get to ditch them for a couple of hours). We know that putting your kids in day care might not fit into the image of the ideal mother that you have in your head. What are your worries about putting your kids in day care?

_____

_____

_____

_____

_____

Now, it's time to let those worries go. There is no evidence that kids who are in day care when they're young do any worse than other kids. Further, studies show that kids who are in day care when they're young may develop better socialization skills.[12] So relax, day care won't ruin your children.

What if your kids hate day care? First, are there changes you could make: investigating other day-care programs, trying to find one of your kids' friends to go to the same day care, or rewarding good behavior at day care with incentives that your kid wants?

_____

_____

_____

_____

_____

But if those don't work for your situation, don't sweat it. It's normal for kids to hate things sometimes. Marina's parents both worked full-time growing up, and everyday she went to an after-school program. She doesn't remember liking it that much. But she learned how to play handball from one of the older kids in the program, and that was how she made friends when she transitioned to a new school years later.

Think back: weren't there things your parents made you do that you hated? Didn't you get over it?

_____

_____

_____

_____

_____

_____

Your kids will, too. And they will probably learn something along the way.

4

Avoiding the Tug of War

Sometimes gender bias against women fuels a Tug of War among women.

"There's a special place in hell for women who don't support other women," Madeleine Albright famously said.[1] We're not sure we agree, actually. Championing other women can be politically costly. Men don't have to take a position on social inequality in order to be successful in their careers, and it's a pretty heavy backpack to carry. We don't think women should have to, either.

We admire women who choose to help other women but don't feel women have some special obligation to actively advocate for other women. But that's different from aligning with men against other women. This strikes us as creepy. Moreover, studies show that women who align with other women tend to be more successful than women who don't.[2]

Take time to reflect. Do women at your workplace tend to support each other? If they do, how do they? If they don't, how does that play out?

_____

_____

_____

_____

_____

_____

Most of the dynamics that produce the Tug of War cannot be fixed by fixing women, but a few can. Here are some things to keep in mind.

She's Not Walking the Tightrope Right!

Remember the Tightrope? Women have to walk a narrow path between being seen as too feminine to be competent and too masculine to be likable. This problem is confounded when women start to judge each other.

"No wonder she doesn't get ahead with that little girl voice!" (She's too feminine.)

"No wonder no one likes her. She's a royal bitch!" (She's too masculine.)

Do you see any of this going on at your workplace?

_____

_____

_____

_____

_____

_____

If you find yourself doing this, just cut it out. It's a signal that all women at that particular workplace are on a tightrope, trying to negotiate a narrow range of acceptable behavior with just the right balance of masculine and feminine traits. Typically, men aren't required to do this, which gives them a natural advantage.

Before you judge, remember that you're on the Tightrope, too!

She's a Bad Mother! She's a Bad Worker!

Another common pattern is for mothers to criticize other mothers for balancing work and family incorrectly in order to assuage their guilt.

Same message: you not only need to stop judging yourself for being a bad mother because you work or work too much. You also need to give other mothers a break. Remember, mothers are walking a tightrope with a stroller—we're all trying to find some acceptable balance between being an ideal worker and being an ideal mother. We all make compromises as a result.

Let her do it her way. You do it yours.

📖 (Read with *What Works*, pages 198–200, to help you think this through.)

PART II

Getting the Job You Want

5

Finding Your Dream Job?

Your Two- to Five-Year Plan

What you want is not your dream job but your next job. Just as the surest way to get writer's block is to insist that the first sentence you write has to be more brilliant than David Foster Wallace, the surest path to despair is to spend forever looking for that *perfect* job. What you need is your next job, not your perfect job—a job that gets you one step closer to your ideal career.

To plot a path, you need to know where you're going. What would you like to be doing in seven to ten years?

_____

_____

_____

_____

_____

_____

What if you don't know? If you don't know, do some research and develop some possibilities. *What Color Is Your Parachute?* by Richard Bolles is a good place to start. For some people, figuring out what you want to do is difficult; others have known since birth. For Marina, she graduated college clear on what *type* of work she wanted to do: social justice and advocacy work, research and writing, maybe something in the nonprofit sector? But she wasn't clear on what that job was or where she should begin to look for it. That's where informational interviews are so important: finding people whose careers appeal to you and using their experience to help you decide if that career might be something you want to try and how to do it.

Informational Interviews
Finding People
So how do you find people to talk with you? Cold calling or e-mails might work, but that's like winning the lottery. You need to figure out how to find links to someone who might be helpful to you. Some possibilities:

1. Someone you already know.
2. Someone a family member or friend knows.
3. Someone who graduated from your college, high school, or other school. Often colleges have formal alumni networks. Does yours? If so, use it.
4. Someone you share another affiliation with: church, club, or the like.
5. A friend of a friend. Use LinkedIn to find out who knows someone who might be helpful to you. (For more tips for using LinkedIn, go to chapter 6 in the workbook.)

Write down at least three people you will ask for an informational interview.

1. _____
2. _____
3. _____
4. _____
5. _____

In what order should you talk with them? Save the most influential people for last to optimize your chances of making a good impression. Start with someone you feel you have more leeway with to ask what might seem like a beginner's question. List the order you'll talk with people in:

1. _____
2. _____
3. _____
4. _____
5. _____

What to Say in an Informational Interview

You have four basic goals:

1. To express interest and enthusiasm for what they do: "I think I may want to be just like you" is a flattering thing for people to hear and will predispose them toward helping you. If you don't know if you want to be like them, consider it a thought experiment and talk yourself into this frame of mind.
2. To find out how they spend their days and figure out whether that appeals to you.
3. To figure out what the career arc looks like in their line of work and how they got to where they are today.
4. To discover any challenges you feel their career has held. If you're worried about something, you need to find someone you feel comfortable surfacing that issue with.

Keep in mind, if you are sincerely interested in someone and express enthusiasm for what they do, they will tend to think of you as a person with good taste—because you are interested in them!

Okay, now write out three to five questions to ask during your informational interviews.

1. _____

2. _____

3. _____

4. _____

5. _____

Work-Life Balance

What if the job you really want leaves a lot to be desired in terms of work-life balance—and that's really important to you? Don't give up on something you really want to do because of work-life balance concerns. Often a job will open up possibilities you can't even imagine from where you sit today. On the other hand, if you are equally interested in two different careers, and one is better in terms of work-life balance, then it's just a more appealing job. Chapter 27 in the workbook has more on work-life balance.

Do Your Homework

Every time you talk about your career with other people, you are developing relationships that could be helpful to you in the future. Impress them. Make sure you do your research so that you sound knowledgeable. Now write out two to three questions you will ask to show them that you have really made an effort to understand what they do. See chapter 9 in the workbook for more on this.

_____

_____

_____

_____

_____

_____

6

Make Social Media Work for You

Your presence on social media can be an effective tool for you to build your network and land your dream job. Or it could be the reason your network remains small and recruiters haven't reached out to you yet. Here are some dos, don'ts, tips, and tricks for making social media work for you.

LinkedIn

If you don't yet have a LinkedIn page, go make one right now. These days, everyone has a LinkedIn page. The bartender at Marina's neighborhood dive bar has a LinkedIn page.

If you already have a LinkedIn page, pull it up on your computer and review your profile:

a. When was the last time you updated your profile?

_____

b. How many connections do you have?

_____

c. Of those connections, approximately what percentage are random people you don't know?

_____

d. How do you feel about your LinkedIn profile and presence? Confident? Unsure? Like it needs work?

_____

_____

_____

e. Have you ever gotten a job opportunity through LinkedIn?

_____

We'll work on all these questions during this section. First, we'll go over how to create a strong profile that works for you and your specific needs. Then we'll discuss how to use your profile to enhance and further your career.

Step 1: Your Photo

Your main LinkedIn profile picture is important, as it's the first thing people look at when they visit your page. Your photo should be a headshot-type picture, and you should use the same picture across different platforms: your company's website, your other social media outlets, and any self-promotion materials you create. This way, you maintain brand consistency (yes, you are a brand) and make it easier for people to recognize and follow you online. For example, this is Joan's LinkedIn picture (this is also her picture on WorkLifeLaw.org and on academic directories, and it's what she gives to conferences she speaks at to use in their materials):

Why is this photo effective?

- The background is not distracting, and it doesn't compete with her face for attention. (We're sure you had fun at Disneyland, but your profile picture doesn't need to reflect that.)
- It is a simple headshot. The rest of your profile should reflect all the activities that you do—your picture shouldn't.
- Joan is the only one in the picture (and she didn't crop anybody else out). Your absolute favorite picture of yourself might be when you posed with your family at Thanksgiving last year, but don't use that for your profile picture. Use your second-favorite photo of yourself, where you stand alone.
- Smile! (or Don't) Lots of people recommend that you smile in your profile picture, as it conveys warmth and personality. We agree that it helps to convey warmth and personality, but that doesn't mean you have to have a cheesy wide-grin smile.

Step 2: Crafting Your Perfect Headline

This is the sentence directly below your name on your profile page. First, write down what it says currently:

_____

_____

Now, rethink your sentence in terms of creating a "professional tagline"[1] for yourself. It should be snappy and concise but also detailed! If you are an associate in a law firm, don't just say "associate in X Law Firm." Instead, include your area of law, your specialty, and your committee memberships: "Licensing and IP attorney experienced in intellectual property disputes, current Director of Technology and Innovation Committee." If you are a student, include your field of study, your past experiences, and your goals: "Masters in Public Policy candidate with experience in X, Y, Z, seeking opportunities in political policy mapping and lobbying."

Rewrite your sentence, adding more detailed descriptions with the least amount of words possible:

_____

_____

Next, think of adding adjectives to your headline that describe your work ethic. Reflect on how past co-workers or friends have described you, and try to bring one or two into your headline—for example, "Detail-oriented marketing firm associate with creative portfolio interested in new-media advertising strategies." Rewrite your headline using at least one adjective:

_____

_____

Recruiters have told us that headlines on LinkedIn are critical, so try to make yours as distinctive and personal as possible.

Step 3: Detail-ify Your Profile

Unlike on your resume, which needs to be concise, LinkedIn is an appropriate place for you to expound on your career and interests. Adding detail helps recruiters and potential clients learn more about you and your past accomplishments. It also helps build your credibility and boosts your professional image.

Consider your current job. Take a couple of minutes and write out everything that you do at your job—literally everything you can think of that you do as part of your job or have done once for your company, not leaving anything out (you might need an extra sheet):

_____

_____

_____

_____

_____

_____

_____

_____

_____

_____

_____

Now think of the main skills or accomplishments that you want to get across on your LinkedIn page. Think about your future dream job: what piece of your story do you want your current job to tell? List the three main takeaways you want readers to get from your profile:

1. _____

_____

2. _____

_____

3. _____

_____

Now, review your list of everything you do at your job and write out the things that best reflect the main takeaways that you identified. For example, if one of your takeaways is that you want to prove that you have experience managing high-profile clients, pull out everything you listed that relates to finding, securing, and managing clients. If you also pioneered casual Fridays at your office, maybe leave that out, as it doesn't help prove your case that you can manage high-profile clients. Write these out below:

1. _____

_____

2. _____

_____

3. _____

_____

These are the details that you should include on your LinkedIn page. Repeat this process for your previous jobs, so your LinkedIn page now contains details about your professional career that promote your work in the way that you want.

Step 4: Tips and Tricks

✓ *Add "projects" to your profile*, in addition to the details we worked out before. Adding projects is a strategic way to add color and substance to your job history by giving people specific examples of your accomplishments. In addition, they can help your network by tagging the people whom you worked with.

✓ *Turn your notifications off!* On your profile page, you'll see a box called "Notify Your Network," and the default position is "Yes." This means that every time you change anything on your profile, it will be publicized to your entire network. People will be very annoyed by this! Turn this option to "No" but consider strategically turning it on when making big changes (such as announcing a new job or adding a big project you worked on).

✓ *Customize your URL!* Make the URL link to your LinkedIn simple and easy to remember, without all those annoying numbers. Because LinkedIn changes its platform routinely, search the Internet for "how to change your LinkedIn URL" if you can't figure it out. If your name is uncommon, we suggest just using your full name (linkedin.com/YourName). If that's taken, try adding your middle initial or full middle name. If those are taken, consider adding your initials (linkedin.com/JoanCWilliamsJCW) or your birthday (linkedin.com/JoanCWilliams24).

✓ Put your customized LinkedIn URL on your resume so people can easily learn more about you.

✓ Once you're satisfied with your profile, *keep it public.* This way, even if people aren't connected with you, like recruiters, they can find you and view your page.

Step 5: Dos and Don'ts

DO! Use language that mirrors the type of work that you're interested in. Literally. If you find a job posting that you really want, use the exact same words to describe yourself as it uses to describe the position. This will make it easier for recruiters in that space to find you. You can always change it later.

DO! Routinely update your LinkedIn profile. Even if you aren't actively searching for a new job, it helps to keep your LinkedIn updated with your latest projects and accomplishments.

DON'T! Update your profile once and then forget about it forever. It will make getting it up-to-date so much harder in the future when you start a job hunt. And chances are you will forget a lot of the things you did if you wait months or years in between updates.

DO! Use LinkedIn to stay connected to your network. Pay attention to the recent updates in your networks—when people get a new job, leave a job, have a work anniversary, birthday, and so on. When appropriate, send people little messages of congratulations; this will keep you in their minds down the road. These small touches can help solidify your professional relationships.

DON'T! Send people the generic message that LinkedIn suggests. *Make sure to personalize these requests!* It only takes a second, but adding a personal line in addition to or instead of the LinkedIn suggested message makes it exponentially more personal and genuine. See part 3, "Networks," on how to craft these messages.

DO! Inventory your connections. Go through your connections pages and map your connections; are they from college, graduate school, professional acquaintances, past jobs? Write down the group and then approximately how many contacts you have from each:

Group title: _____

Number of contacts: _____

Group title: _____

Number of contacts: _____

Group title: _____

Number of contacts: _____

Group title: _____

Number of contacts: _____

Group title: _____

Number of contacts: _____

Review this map. Are you particularly heavy in one area and lacking in another? Are there a lot of random people whom you don't know? Where are the holes in your professional network? Use this as a map for how you accept requests for connections and seek out connections going forward.

DON'T! Accept LinkedIn requests from random people you don't know, unless you have an affiliation with them (you both worked at the same firm, went to the same school, or the like). A truly random LinkedIn connection won't help you advance your career.

Step 6: Using LinkedIn to Help Your Career

Think about LinkedIn as a space to develop and advertise your personal brand (that would be you). Your profile picture, profile details, and tagline all help shape your brand. Now you need to get it out there.

What is your personal brand? For example, "I'm a tech entrepreneur that wants to use technological innovation to fuel social change." Write down yours:

_____

_____

_____

_____

_____

Who are the target audiences that you're trying to reach? It could be broad like "change agents in Silicon Valley" or specific companies or investment groups that you know of.

_____

_____

_____

_____

_____

_____

Identify areas of mutual interest between your personal brand and your target audiences. If your target audience is broad—"change agents in Silicon Valley"—what are they going to be interested in? Where do they get their news? What issues do they follow closely? (If you don't know, whom could you ask? See chapter 5 in the workbook for informational interviews and part 4, "Networks"). If your target audience is very specific—"XY Investments"—who are their clients? What have been their greatest successes?

_____

_____

_____

_____

_____

_____

All this will help you post content on LinkedIn that will help you get noticed by the people you're targeting and will put you in association with the community that you want to work in. Posting content can change your LinkedIn experience from being passive ("Oh poo, no one added me today") to active ("Watch me drive people and business to my page!").

If you're a filmmaker and you finish editing a new trailer, post it! If you're a web designer and you made your best friend's wedding website, post it! If you're traveling for a work event, post where you are and the event you're attending! You get the gist: anything you do that is sharable that helps promote your personal brand, post it! These types of updates can lead to job opportunities.[2]

Note: Hopefully this goes without saying, but don't treat your LinkedIn like your Twitter account. Be conscious of the frequency with which you update and limit the content to work-related topics that will further your brand (not what you had for lunch—unless maybe you're a chef!).

Identify three things coming down the pipeline in the next month or two that you could write an update about:

_____

_____

_____

_____

_____

_____

Another great, low-key way to update is to selectively share other people's posts. Think of yourself as a curator for your personal exhibit of the LinkedIn museum. Share other people's materials that reflect the brand you are creating. Refer back to the target audiences you identified and your mutual interest areas and post content that fits. Repost content that your target audiences post, adding a line with your personal take. Doing so can put you in association with the crowd you're trying to run with.

More Tips
- ✓ If you want to work for a particular company, follow it on LinkedIn! Look at what issues the company follows and follow those too.
- ✓ Post content (blog post, news article, opinion piece) that relates to the company's mission and tag the company in it.
- ✓ Use LinkedIn to find who the higher-ups are in the company and see if you have any mutual connections. Connecting with someone who doesn't know you, especially if they are more advanced than you, probably won't help you that much. Finding someone who could make a connection between the two of you would go much further.

Facebook

Everyone has that friend on Facebook who posts way too much, about stuff that is way too boring, way too often. You do not want to be this person. Studies show that frequent/unimportant posting is the number-one reason why people get defriended.[3] Instead of sharing everything that comes to mind or every picture you take, think strategically about the purpose of your Facebook presence and your intended audience.

First, why do you have a Facebook? Is it for your personal use, to keep up with friends? Or is it to help you professionally?

_____

_____

_____

_____

_____

If your answer included a little of both reasons, get strategic about your privacy settings. You can create sublists within your friends and then customize which group you want to see which of your posts. For example, create a sublist of your friends that you work with, a different sublist of people you went to law school with, and another sublist of people you play soccer with on the weekends. Then, when you go to post a braggy article about how Arsenal beat Chelsea 3–0 in the Champion's League, you can share it only with people who would appreciate your post (your soccer friends), while not outing yourself as an obsessed British soccer fan to your workplace.

Does this work with your Facebook friends? Identify subgroups of your friends that you could create:

_____

_____

_____

_____

_____

Sharing different posts with different people can help to limit your Facebook presence (if you tend to be an oversharer), and it can also help you craft the image you want to project professionally, while still speaking out about what matters to you personally.

Posting about politics and social issues is risky, so if you have strong opinions about an issue, share your posts only with your "close friend" sublist or maybe your "college" sublist. Don't censor yourself but protect yourself from potential workplace backlash by keeping work and politics separate. (Same goes for strong opinions on any of the Kardashians.)

If you're someone who mostly uses Facebook for strictly social reasons, consider including some work and professional content in your Facebook life. It can be a good platform to share things like interesting articles or upcoming events—things that relate to your work but that wouldn't necessarily be appropriate for your LinkedIn page. But while an interesting article on the practice of rural law might not benefit your day-to-day life at a busy city law firm, people in the field might think it's interesting and might think *you're* a more interesting person for having that perspective.

Facebook can be a useful way to show off more aspects of your personality than LinkedIn allows for. And if you have an interesting Facebook presence that people pay attention to, they are more likely to pay attention if you post asking for leads on new jobs or asking for feedback on a company that's scouting you.

7

Writing Your Resume and Acing the Interview

Now you know what kind of job you want, and you're trying to land it. If you're like most people, you'll lose out on jobs you really wanted and on jobs you really think you should have gotten. There are two basic principles to getting a job without losing your mind:

1. **Remember, you only need one job.** That means you can lose out on a lot of jobs without having it affect your life at all.
2. **A key factor in who becomes successful is resilience.** Don't dwell on the jobs you didn't get. You most likely will never know why you didn't get them. Don't ruminate about what you could have done differently or whether the decision was fair. Just move on. *Behind every successful person is a string of failures.* What made them successful is that they didn't give up.

The remainder of this chapter will help you write a great resume and ace the interview. Both contexts, though, present Tightrope challenges. Let's introduce those here first.

Gender Judo?

You need to show your value, so you highlight your accomplishments in a direct, no-nonsense way. Alas, sometimes this is all it takes to lose a job you really, really want.

As we said, women at work often find themselves walking a Tightrope between being seen as too masculine to be likable and too feminine to be competent. This Tightrope can affect women applying for jobs in several ways.

Women's resumes may trigger backlash if they're seen as bragging. An ambitious man "knows his own worth." A woman who behaves the same way may be seen as a "shameless self-promoter." So annoying: in contexts where men can be direct and no-nonsense, a woman who follows their example may be seen as "difficult" or "not a team player" by someone who expects women to be helpmates who are always to be attuned to the comfort level of those around them. (Note to Future Self: When you're the boss, encourage women to brag all the live-long day about their accomplishments. Chances are they deserve to.)

If you're looking for a job, you can take one of two possible attitudes toward prescriptive gender bias:

1. **"Forget it, keep your sorry-ass job, sexist pig."** Ignore the risk, on the grounds that you wouldn't want to work there anyway if people are going to insist on jamming you into stereotypes. Sometimes conforming to traditionalist expectations would make a woman feel self-estranged. Take the Las Vegas bartender who quit her job rather than wear makeup, as the employer required, because she "felt very degraded and very demeaned" by the makeup requirement; "it affected [her] self-dignity," and she felt that it "took away [her] credibility as an individual and as a person."[1] No job is worth this.

2. **Try to control for backlash.** On the other hand, sometimes you just really need the job. Or you feel comfortable fine-tuning the way you self-present. After all, masculinity and femininity both encapsulate important facets of human potential, and some women feel comfortable returning to the toolkit of masculinity to make themselves seem more credible or the toolkit of femininity to make themselves seem more likable. This is gender judo: mixing the masculine and the feminine to avoid the twin pitfalls of Tightrope bias.

Writing a Great Resume

All this plays out when you write a resume. The key risk concerns self-promotion. Women risk pushback for self-promotion due to prescriptive stereotypes that women are supposed to be modest, self-effacing team players. A man may have to go all the way to Donald Trumping it before he's seen as clearly over the line (and clearly, even then it may not be a deal breaker, hence our president). The range of behavior accepted in women may be far narrower. Here's a resume that goes way too far in the direction of womanly modesty. (*See* pages 56–58.)

Nicki Minaj's Resume #1: Too Modest

Onika Tanya Maraj
Saint James, Trinidad and Tobago
o.maraj@hotmail.com

Education:
LaGuardia High School, Manhattan
No college education

Experience:
Server, Red Lobster, New York
Administrative Assistant, customer service
Office Manager, Wall Street
Rapper, *Playtime Is Over*, 2007
Rapper, *Pink Friday*, 2010
Judge, *American Idol*, 2012
Actress, *The Other Woman*, 2014
Rapper, *The PinkPrint*, 2014

Skills:
Rapping
Singing

Information from Wikipedia.

Here's a resume that goes too far in the Trump direction.

Nicki Minaj's Resume #2: Too Boastful

Nicki Minaj
BAD BITCH Inc., Earth
TheFiercestQueen@nickiminaj.com

Education:
I don't need education; I spit fiercer rhymes than anyone.
I didn't learn how to be me, I just AM. You can't teach this!

Experience:
2007: Crushed the game with my first mix tape, *Playtime Is Over*.
2010: My first album came out and changed the world. People called me the best female rapper, the best rapper ever, the fiercest bitch in show business. My single "Super Bass" is literally the best song ever written.
2011: Continued to RULE THE WORLD.
2012: DOMINATED the MTV VMAs.
2013: *American Idol* begged me to be a judge. I did it, but Mariah Carey is crazy and COULDN'T HANDLE MY TALENT. That show was too small for me anyway.
2013: BROKE ALL THE RECORDS. TRAILBLAZED. SHUT DOWN THE HATERS.
2014: Released my second album, *The PinkPrint*, and it SHATTERED ALL EXPECTATIONS. It won too many awards to count. I had to build a whole new floor in one of my houses to hold all my awards.

Skills:
—Having the flyest style out there. I take fashion risks, I make fashion, I break fashion. Anna Wintour loves me. She calls me all the time. I sit first row at fashion shows, and everyone looks at me instead of the models.
—Being the best rapper in the world. My style is unique, it is sensational. No one has ever heard anything like it. My flow is intense, it's deep, it's inspirational.
—Working with all kinds of people. Everyone in the industry wants to work with me. The top producers, rappers, artists, money makers, they all want me. They call me all the time, begging to work with me. It's because every track I put a verse on is gold.

Information from Wikipedia.

Here's one that's just right. Notice how she gets her accomplishments out by citing objective data, instead of characterizing her own accomplishments: show it, don't say it.

Nicki Minaj's Resume #3: Just Right

Nicki Minaj
MyPinkFriday.com
Young Money Records

Education:
LaGuardia High School: I auditioned and was accepted to the performance arts program at LaGuardia High School.

Experience:
Playtime Is Over (2007), *Sucka Free* (2008): I released my first two mix tapes on Dirty Money Entertainment. I was named Female Artist of the Year at the 2008 Underground Music Awards.
Pink Friday (2010): After signing with Young Money Entertainment, I made my first full-length album, which debuted at No. 2 on the *Billboard* 200 chart. I became the first female solo artist to have seven songs on the *Billboard* Hot 100 simultaneously.
Pink Friday: Roman Reloaded (2012): I released my second studio album, which debuted at No. 1 on the *Billboard* 200 chart. The album's success allowed me to headline my own tour and win the MTV VMA Award for Best Female Video.
PinkPrint (2014): My third studio album focused a lot more on my hip hop roots and continued the conversation of my first two albums. The second single, "Anaconda," became the highest charting single of my career and broke the VEVO record for most views in a single day. I became the only artist to win the BET award for Best Female Hip-Hop Artist six times in a row. At the end of the year, I was nominated for two Grammy Awards, for Best Rap Song and Best Pop Duo/Group Performance.

Skills:
—Asked to front the Viva Glam campaign in 2013.
—Conceptualized, designed, and produced the Nicki Minaj Collection for Kmart, featuring clothing, accessories, and housewares.
—Designed and launched three commercially successful fragrance lines.
—Fronted the spring/summer 2015 Roberto Cavalli campaign.

Information from Wikipedia.

Acing the Interview

Congratulations! You've got an interview. The most important step is to make sure you sound knowledgeable about the organization you are trying to join. It's flattering to your interviewer that you are interested in something they presumably care a lot about—their workplace. It signals both that you are truly interested in the job and that you have good research skills, judgment, and work ethic when you take the time to do extensive research on the organization you are seeking to join.

Don't spend hours memorizing every initiative or project the organization has ever been involved in. Instead, use its website to identify the three main things that the organization prides itself on and think of a couple things to say about them. (Example: A marketing firm might have gotten a big client recently. Read up a little on the client and make up a sentence or two about why you would be excited to work with that particular client, citing specific reasons and ideas you had.)

List three notable things about the organization and something to say about each one:

1. _____

_____

_____

2. _____

_____

_____

3. _____

_____

_____

Next, try to find someone from your network who is knowledgeable about the organization (if you can't think of anyone, can you think of someone who is in the same field or who used to be?). Ask them to highlight for you what is valued most in the organization: Is brilliance or teamwork valued more? Creativity or work ethic? Risk-taking or delivery of work on deadline? When you have a sense for the values of the company, you can advocate for yourself in the right ways.

Finally, think through your strategy for presenting yourself, keeping in mind the values of the company. If it values brilliance over teamwork, spend more time highlighting your accomplishments rather than expressing how exciting it would be to work with your prospective new co-workers.

Bias-Proof Your Interview Style

Assuming you want to do so, now it's time for gender judo. Remember that women are supposed to be modest . . . so how are you supposed to get the word out about your accomplishments? And women are supposed to be attuned to other people's comfort levels . . . so how can you let the dimwit who's interviewing you know you are brilliant without being seen as a prima donna? (Note to Future Self: When you're in a position of power, if you ever hear that dimwit interviewer accuse a woman of being a prima donna, step in and correct them. Or maybe put a fake spider in their desk drawer.)

Here are some straightforward ways you can try to control for backlash.

IF YOU TEND FEMMY . . .

If you marked mostly qualities that are coded as feminine in the "Gender Judo" exercise in the introduction, then you can work to ensure you come off as authoritative.

Describe a time when you felt you were undercut by displaying feminine qualities:

_____

_____

_____

_____

_____

_____

Describe how you could raid the toolkit of masculinity to make yourself seem more authoritative. What are the masculine qualities you feel you could both tolerate and pull off?

_____

_____

_____

_____

_____

Now think specifically about your interview style. What are ways you speak or present yourself that are stereotypically feminine?

_____

_____

_____

_____

_____

_____

How could you enhance your authoritativeness by adopting some qualities from the masculine toolbox?

_____

_____

_____

_____

_____

IF YOU TEND TO BE MORE MASCULINE . . .

If you marked mostly qualities that are coded as masculine in the "Gender Judo" exercise in the introduction, then you can work to ensure you come off as approachable.

Describe a time when you felt you were disliked or seen as abrasive because you had displayed masculine qualities:

_____

_____

_____

_____

_____

Describe how you could raid the toolkit of femininity to make yourself seem more approachable. Steer clear of any feminine quality that could undercut the perception that you are competent, like being giggly, flirty, or deferential. What are the feminine qualities you feel you could both tolerate and pull off?

_____

_____

_____

_____

_____

_____

Good luck! The single most important thing you can do is to sound knowledgeable and to convey enthusiasm. Remember that the people who interview you will typically be invested in the organization you are seeking to join. If you convey that you agree that where they have chosen to work is *great*, they will think you have impeccable judgment!

8

Negotiating Starting Salary

There was a study that asked men and women to describe how they felt about negotiating salaries by comparing it to other activities.[1] Men compared negotiating salaries to "winning a ballgame" or "a wrestling match": in other words, they associated salary negotiation with fun, exciting sports. Women associated it with "going to the dentist." Needless to say, there is a real gap between men's and women's experiences negotiating salaries. In this chapter, we'll try to explain why this is and give you some techniques to make salary negotiating less anxiety provoking and more beneficial to you.

First, write down your top-three anxieties about negotiating your salary. (If you don't feel anxious about it, skip this section and use the time to call the Center for WorkLife Law and tell us your secrets: 415–565–4640).

1. _____

_____

_____

2. _____

_____

_____

3. _____

_____

_____

If you're anything like us (or the many women we've spoken with), your anxieties probably center around not wanting to appear rude or overly greedy to your new employer, who you're very excited and grateful to be working for. You would probably rather just skip the negotiation altogether and accept whatever pay they offer.

Which, if you did, you wouldn't be alone. You've probably heard that "women don't ask": one study found that female business-school students were eight times less likely to negotiate starting salary than their male colleagues were.[2]

But the cost of not negotiating your starting salary can be high and can have long-term consequences. Another study found that negotiating your starting salary can increase your salary 7–10 percent over a lifetime.[3] A different way to think about this is that *not* negotiating your starting salary can cost you around $600,000 in lost earnings over your career.[4] You know the men in your company are getting their $600,000 and will wave at you as they drive past in their new Teslas.

Here are some other reasons to negotiate your starting salary:

1. It sets your pay scale in your new organization, which influences all your future opportunities for promotion, raises, and bonuses.
2. It can influence your pay in future jobs.
3. Most employers expect new hires to negotiate their salary. We have heard managers actually rethink their decision to hire someone after that person accepted the first number offered. (This can also differ by field.)

You may not have heard *why* women don't negotiate. Well, one study found that, if they do, women are more likely to be disliked and less likely to be hired.[5] A man who negotiates hard is showing he's competitive and ambitious—"a man to be reckoned with." But a woman who is competitive and ambitious is not living up to prescriptive stereotypes that the good woman is modest, self-effacing, and nice. (Note to Future Self: When you're in a position to hire awesome women, encourage them to negotiate their salaries. Even if you can't meet them at their target number, let them know that you respect their zeal and don't hold it against them.)

Luckily, one study shows a formula for how to negotiate starting salary without backlash, and we'll walk you through it. But first, you need to prepare.

Delay "The Talk"

If you can avoid it, try not to enter salary negotiations until the offer stage. Why? You want to put yourself in the best bargaining position. If you wait until the offer stage, you can shift the power imbalance more in your favor. At the point that an employer is offering you a job, it is invested in you. It has determined that you are the best candidate for the job, and it has invested time into interviewing you, checking your references, and thinking seriously about what you have to offer. It doesn't want to go back to the drawing board with a candidate it didn't like as much. Which means you have some power in the situation, and you should use it to your advantage.

How do you delay the talk? First, cover your tracks. If there is a question about salary on an application, don't put in a number. If there's room, write in something like "reasonable market price" or "prefer to discuss at offer stage." If it's a form application that requires a number, write a dash ("—").

Sometimes employers want to talk about salary during your interview. Prepare for this beforehand by prepping vague responses:

✓ "I'll consider any reasonable offer."
✓ "I'm still learning about the role and your organization, and I would have a much better sense of the appropriate salary later in the hiring process, once I

have a better understanding about what the job entails."

✓ "I'm not so much concerned with pay package than with learning about your organization. If it's okay, I'd like to use my limited time to hear more about the role and discuss salary later in the process."

Spend a couple of minutes practicing similar responses that feel comfortable to you and write down one that you like:

_____

_____

_____

_____

_____

Do Your Homework

In most situations, negotiating your starting salary is appropriate—even expected—when you accept a new job. But in certain situations, salaries are fixed, and trying to negotiate for a higher salary won't work. Unions, minimum wage, and grant funding are a couple of factors that sometimes make salaries nonnegotiable.

If you're not sure if your salary is negotiable, try to identify someone in the know whom you could ask. Was there someone in the interview process you felt like you really clicked with, who's not in charge of your salary, whom you could ask?

_____

_____

If there's not, do you know anyone who's in the field, who maybe had a similar position at a similar company before?

_____

_____

Next, find out how much your job is worth. There are two main ways to find out approximately how much you should be making in your job.

First, do some online research. There are many websites that can help. Here are a couple we've found (as we all know, websites come and go, but at the time of this writing, these sites were up and running):

Salary.com	www.salary.com	Enter your job title and your city of employment and get a free quote of the median salary for other jobs like yours in the area. Paid option releases more detailed reports.
Payscale.com	www.payscale.com	Create an anonymous profile with your salary, details about your employer, and the region you work in and see where you rank in terms of salary and benefits with comparable people in your field.
Glassdoor.com	www.glassdoor.com	Compare your pay and benefits to others in your field. Also access information about the culture and work environment of different companies.
Occupational Outlook Handbook	www.bls.gov	Go to "Subjects" and then "Wages by Area and Occupation." Includes information on required education and certifications.
SimplyHired	www.simplyhired.com	See average salaries for your job in your area and compare your salary to others in similar jobs nationally.

Second, reach out to your network. Do you know anyone working in the field whom you could have a frank conversation with about salary?

_____

_____

_____

_____

_____

Do you know anyone in the field who is maybe more senior but who started out at the level you're entering? (The economy has changed, but you can still get a general idea.)

_____

_____

_____

_____

_____

Figure Out Your Numbers

What is the absolute rock-bottom number that you can accept? What is your target salary? These numbers should be based on the homework you did above and some basic calculations about what you need to live on.

What Is Your Rock-Bottom Number?

To figure this out, factor in your monthly expenses (rent, bills, food, etc.) and, if applicable, consult with your partner on what your family can live on:

_____

_____

_____

_____

_____

What is your target salary?

_____

It's important to have these numbers figured out ahead of time and to tell yourself that you are going to stick to them. When you're in the heat of negotiations, you may feel pressured to say yes, even if the number seems low to you. You don't want to walk out of the meeting with a job you want on a salary you can't eat on. If the employer is not budging on a number that is below your rock-bottom number, it may be more prudent for you and your family to walk away. Walking away from a job interview, unless you are desperate, should always be an option.

Don't *Give a Range!*

Just don't do it! Offering a range may be tempting, especially for women, as a way to seem more reasonable and out of fear that you may be asking for too much. Resist this temptation. It is a trap. Why? First of all, it lets you off the hook for asking for what you really want. If you know your target salary but think it's a little high and are scared to ask for it, offering a range with your target in the middle (or even worse, at the top) lets you wiggle out of the discomfort of negotiating. Don't do this! Work through the exercises in this section, do your homework, have your facts ready, ask for what you want, and be ready to back it up. Second of all, why on earth would an employer ever give you more than the bottom of your range? If your target is $60,000, and you tell your employer that your range is $55,000–$65,000, they are most likely going to offer you $55,000, and you won't be in a space to negotiate because you already told them that you are okay with $55,000. You don't leave yourself any room to negotiate.

That's why we advise women to figure out their target salary and their bottom line beforehand: to have a mental range. Ask for your target salary, don't tell them about your bottom line, and keep that range in your head.

Practice

There may be tough questions asked during negotiations. The best way to prepare for these is to practice them.

What are the top-three questions about salary that you're afraid of?

1. _____

_____

_____

2. _____

_____

_____

3. _____

_____

_____

Now prepare some responses to these questions. Here's an example:

Q: "The number you're asking for is more than we paid the person in the position before you. Why should we give more money to someone we don't know will work out?"

A: "I think the experience and training I will bring to the position will expand the scope of what can be accomplished in this role. I am ready to commit to bringing the company to new levels, and I'd like my salary to reflect this expanded vision."

Write down your responses below. Focus on highlighting the unique things you bring to the table and how those qualities will benefit the organization you're joining.

1. _____

_____

_____

2. _____

_____

_____

3. _____

_____

_____

It's important to remember that if you're not sure, you can always ask for more time. If the employer's representatives are pressuring you to accept a number you're not totally comfortable with, say you need a day or two to think it over or say you are waiting to hear back from another position and you will get back to them in a few days. They may say no, but it also may encourage them to offer you your target salary in the name of closing the deal. Don't say you need time to talk it over with your partner or husband. That may well be true, but it can signal that you're not the one calling the shots in your career.

Practice a few responses that buy you time to think:

1. _____

_____

_____

2. _____

_____

_____

3. _____

_____

_____

Prep Your Brag List

You want to be ready to show, not just tell, the employer why you should be paid your target salary. Prep a list of accomplishments, relevant experience, and unique qualifications that make you well suited for the role. (See chapter 12 in the workbook for how to keep and develop this list.)

Write them down here:

_____

_____

_____

_____

_____

_____

Now, pick your top three and write down why they will benefit the organization that you hope to join. Try to make it as specific as possible. Here's an example:

Brag point: "I raised annual giving by 15 percent in one year at my last company."
Benefit: "In addition to the strategic direction I will bring, my effectiveness at fund-
raising will help secure the program's future and expand into X market."

Write down your three top brag points that will benefit the organization you are interviewing with:

1. _____

_____

_____

2. _____

_____

_____

3. _____

_____

_____

Expand the Pie

Don't limit your research to just salary numbers. In addition to your bottom line and target numbers, consider other forms of benefits and compensation.

Additional Items to Consider
- ✓ Allowances: cleaning, travel, gas
- ✓ Bonuses
- ✓ Commissions
- ✓ Commuter options
- ✓ Company car
- ✓ Education or tuition reimbursement for you and for family members
- ✓ Expense accounts
- ✓ Flexible schedule
- ✓ Health/dental/vision coverage
- ✓ Leave eligibility

✓ Life insurance / other insurance
✓ Off-cycle performance review
✓ Paid sick time
✓ Parental leave
✓ Pay-grade adjustments (move to bottom of higher pay grade, so there is more room to grow)
✓ Professional development opportunities
✓ Relocation assistance
✓ Retirement plan options
✓ Sign-on bonus
✓ Stock options
✓ Telecommuting options
✓ Vacation time / holiday pay

Consider these additional benefits with two strategies in mind: First, if your employer won't budge on salary, you can supplement your base pay with additional benefits. Second, if one or more of these additional benefits are important to your work-life balance (such as having a flexible schedule or being able to take vacation), identify those items as priorities. Which ones are important to your life? Rank the items above: which is at the top? Which is at the bottom? Practice discussing them along with your target salary:

_____

_____

_____

_____

_____

_____

Don't Hate, Negotiate!

The time has finally come. You've interviewed for your job, successfully delayed talks of salary, did your homework, and got offered the job! Congratulations! Now come the negotiations. We have a few guidelines to offer to help you get the salary you want without getting backlash for negotiating as a woman.

1. Come prepared. If you've done your homework, you should be set. The night before, make sure to practice again your responses to the questions you're a little scared of.

2. Don't open. Wait for the employer to offer a starting number. This will give you a better bargaining position and ensure that you don't undercut yourself.

Sometimes the employer will frame the salary number as nonnegotiable. This is where, as a woman, you have to tread carefully in order to avoid backlash. As we discussed, men are expected to negotiate, while women are expected to be deferential.

Luckily, research has shown that if you frame your negotiation carefully, you can avoid backlash.[6] Use the following formulas to open up negotiations:

"It wasn't clear to me whether this represents the top or the bottom of the pay range."

"I don't know how typical it is for people at my level to negotiate salary, but I'm hopeful you'll see my skill at negotiating as something important I'll bring to the team."

"My mentor stressed how important it is to negotiate if there's a pay range. He also stressed I should say I'd like to be eligible for a year-end bonus."

By using these careful framing techniques, you can enter negotiations while still staying in the lane of what's "expected" as a woman.

Now your turn. What will you say if the employer says the salary is nonnegotiable?

_____

_____

_____

_____

_____

_____

If the employer is willing to negotiate but pushes you to open negotiations, try your best impression of an artful dodger:

EMPLOYER: I need to know your target salary to make you an offer. Can you give me a range?

YOU: You're in a much better position to suggest an appropriate range based on your knowledge of what's budgeted for the position and the range for similarly qualified employees in similar roles. Why don't we start the conversation there?

3. Counter with a carefully researched response. Bring in the homework you did, your past earnings, and your qualifications to your counter. Instead of just "How about $75,000?" try "I've done lots of research, and it seems that the average salary for this type of position in this market is between $70,000 and $85,000. So in that context, I think $75,000 is reasonable, especially considering my eight years of experience in this field."

Another tactic: "I was expecting that your offer was going to be around $75,000. This number is lower than I was planning for. I will have to give it some thought."

Don't try to leverage another offer in your counter. Research has shown that this doesn't work for women.[7]

4. If unsure, think on it. Don't accept an offer if you don't want to. If the employer is not budging and the number is too low, ask for more time. See above when you wrote down a couple of lines that will buy you time. At the point when the employer is offering you the job, it is invested in bringing you on board. When you ask for more time, it gives whomever you're negotiating with time to discuss the job and your qualifications with those higher up; hopefully they will come back with a number that's closer to your target.

5. Clinch the deal—then deal some more. Don't forget about nonsalary benefits. Once you've agreed to a number, make sure you also nail down the priority benefits that you identified earlier.

When you've settled on salary and benefits, make sure to write your agreement down and e-mail it to the employer, so you have a record. You can frame it as "I'm excited to be part of such a great company. Thanks for speaking with me today and addressing my concerns. These are my records from our agreement."

How did it go? What's one thing you could do better next time? Was there something you wished you would have prepared for that you hadn't?

_____

_____

_____

_____

_____

_____

Now go have a glass of wine and toast to your new job! (Note to Future Self: Consider instituting Wine Wednesdays when you're in charge.)

PART III

Networks

It's not what you know. It's who you know.

We know you've heard this adage before and are probably sick of it. But you also have probably seen how true it can be.

Building and maintaining a strong network can help you

1. Land a job
2. Excel in your current job
3. Be successful overall

In this part, you'll learn how and why networks can help you in all facets of your life. The trick for working women is to build networks that not only help their careers but support their work lives as well. We are not going to tell you to go out and suck up to a bunch of men whom you don't like, who don't get you, and who say gross things around you, because you probably get enough of that already. Furthermore, a network built of people you don't like won't end up helping you that much. Networks should include the people you trust, the people you rely on, the people whom you can talk to when you need some advice. If everyone in your network is a sexist pig, then you're going to feel very isolated in your network.

Instead, we're going to be strategic about how we build out our networks, both internally within your organization and externally across your professional and personal circles. As a woman, believe it or not, you are in a position of advantage over a lot of men. Why? Because you probably talk to people who aren't men! And because you do, you are in a great position to be a network broker—someone who can connect two (or more) different, otherwise-unconnected networks. And that is the most powerful position to hold.

There are two basic types of networks: clique networks and entrepreneurial networks.

Clique networks are characterized by their strong ties—not just to you and the members of the clique but also between the other members of the clique.[1] Clique networks tend to be insular: members of the clique usually have few ties to other networks. Because of these strong ties, clique networks typically enjoy high levels of trust between members and thus can offer socio-emotional support to their members. From a business standpoint, clique networks are advantageous because members can coordinate easily with each other, transfer complicated information to each other, and help each other with their careers. But clique networks have high redundancy: members mostly only confer with each other, so they have limited access to new information. Clique networks tend to lack diversity in people, ideas, and solutions.

Entrepreneurial networks, by contrast, are characterized by weak and nonredundant ties.[2] For example, let's say you know a couple of people from the marketing team, a couple of people from the policy shop, and a couple of people in the start-up world—but those people don't know each other. The advantages of this type of network is that you get access to lots of different information, from different perspectives, with little redundancy. Further, you can speak more freely with different legs of the entrepreneurial network without the worry that it will get back to you. And if you can connect one or more legs of the network—introduce the marketing people to the start-up people, for example—you become a valuable network broker, working as an essential bridge. The con of entrepreneurial networks is that they lack the tight-knit, trusting types of connections that cliques offer.

Which type of network do you more naturally gravitate toward?

_____

Because of societal norms of friendship, men are more likely to naturally establish back-scratching, entrepreneurial types of networks: you scratch my back, and I'll scratch yours. These types of relationships may feel false for some women, if you're the type who usually develops closer, more intimate relationships. Is that the case for you?

_____

If you feel uncomfortable with back-scratching types of relationships, why do you think that is? If you can help someone and in return they can help you, why not do it?

_____

_____

_____

_____

_____

_____

After all, that's essentially what networking is: you add value for someone, and they add value for you. You'll learn more about this later in this part, as well as tips for how to do this in ways that feel authentic.

9

Making Connections

Let's Analyze Your Network

When you hear the word "network," who are the people in your life that come to mind?

_____

_____

_____

_____

_____

_____

Now look at whom you wrote about: are they work related, personal relationships, or both? Explain:

_____

_____

_____

_____

_____

_____

_____

Let's identify any gaps in your network. Here are a bunch of ways that networks affect both your professional and personal life. After each, write whether you have used your network for this in the past. And if you haven't, write down why.

Has your network helped you to . . .

Get a job?

_____

_____

_____

_____

_____

_____

Manage your staff better or more efficiently?

_____

_____

_____

_____

_____

Hear about work-related opportunities?

_____

_____

_____

_____

_____

Land a client?

_____

_____

_____

_____

_____

Get access to important work information?

_____

_____

_____

_____

_____

_____

Make friends?

_____

_____

_____

_____

_____

Get your kids the right teachers?

_____

_____

_____

_____

_____

Adapt to a new situation?

_____

_____

_____

_____

_____

Make healthy choices or get medical support?

_____

_____

_____

_____

_____

_____

Be happy?

_____

_____

_____

_____

_____

Review what you wrote down. If it seems the main reason why your network hasn't been helping you is because you don't know enough people, focus on the "Making Connections" section.

If you feel you have a good network of people but have a hard time drawing on them, focus on the "Getting the Most Out of Your Network" section.

If you have a good personal network but are not getting the professional benefits out of your work network, focus on the "How Your Work Networks Work" section.

Maybe you're thinking, "Okay, my network hasn't helped me with some of these, but does it really have to? What's so special or important about networks?"

Here's where we bring in a little bit of the findings from social science. If you've ever looked into the science behind networks, you've probably found that there is a huge literature about networks, and much of it is math heavy. Fear not, you needn't do math. But a couple of statistics can help show why networks are so important.

First, success is heavily tied to your network and your ability to create a network.[1] People with better networks tend to have more social capital, and they actually tend to fare better at both work and home.[2]

Second, studies show that between 51 and 70 percent of managers and professionals find jobs through personal contacts.[3] Here's the clincher: at the highest professional levels, that number increases to 90 percent.[4] So if you're a midlevel professional with aspirations of moving up the corporate ladder, your network only grows in importance. Not only does your network play a role in getting a promotion, but it can also affect how effective you are at your job.[5] Landing a job isn't the end goal of building your network—it's only the beginning. Have you landed most of your jobs through connections? Why or why not?

_____

_____

_____

_____

_____

_____

Networks aren't just important for corporate professionals; they are hugely important for working women in all sectors. If you live in a small town or in an area that operates like a small town, connections through friends and family are everything. Sometimes networks are even more important in small towns, as job openings and work issues aren't broadcast through formal channels like HR postings as often. Usually they're just passed around by word of mouth. Frequenting local bars and hangouts can help keep you in the loop. But if barhopping isn't an option—you have kids, or you work nights, or you simply don't like spending your time in bars listening to men complain—that's where having an effective network can really help.

Making Connections

The good news is that networks can seriously help your work and personal life. If you're an outgoing person who likes talking to people and putting yourself out there, then you probably agree that this is good news.

But what if you're an introvert? What if you're the type of person who would rather eat beetles than attend events with names like "mixer," "function," or "cocktail anything"? Introverts find energy in spending time alone and get easily drained by social events. Don't worry, you don't have to change your whole personality. There are lots of different ways that people can build and operate in networks, and your personality type is a big factor in how you do that. Joan is a self-described introvert and skips work social events whenever possible. She also has a huge network, which she draws on regularly, and which she has built and maintained over two decades. There are many different types of networks, and the goal is to help you build and maintain one that works for you.

How do you feel about networking events? Fun? Worse than the dentist?

_____

_____

_____

_____

_____

_____

If you find them less than fun, is this because of a specific experience you had or a general unease of crowds?

_____

_____

_____

_____

_____

_____

Your personality has a lot to do with how you feel about networking. To figure out your personality type (if you don't know it already), we recommend a Myers-Briggs test, which can be accessed online.[6] The test measures personality along four different dichotomies, all of which affect multiple aspects of work. The one we are interested in here is where your personality falls on the Extrovert-Introvert scale.

Are you more of an extrovert or an introvert?

_____

If you're an extrovert, being with other people gives you energy, and you thrive in social situations that others may find uncomfortable. The easy part is getting the contacts. The harder part is following up.

How can you make those first contacts? Go to networking events, mixers, going-away parties, welcome parties, lectures or panels on your area of expertise, office luncheons. List some events you've gone to in the past that you have made connections from:

_____

_____

_____

_____

_____

How successful were you at these events in making connections? Did you swap e-mails or phone numbers? Did you collect business cards?

_____

_____

_____

_____

_____

_____

Here are some pitfalls for extroverts to avoid:

✓ Sometimes, people can be so extroverted and excited to meet new people that they forget to listen super closely to what the other person is saying. Make sure to engage wholeheartedly with everyone you speak with.

✓ If you're at a big event, it can be exciting to scope out the room and see who's there. Make sure when you're speaking with someone, you're not constantly looking over their shoulder at who just walked in the door.

✓ Don't try to talk to everybody. Longer, more in-depth conversations with fewer people will be more helpful in creating lasting and beneficial connections than will short, more surface-level interactions with more people.

If you're an introvert, keep in mind that although you may find large groups of people in large rooms existentially terrifying, there are a couple of ways around that. Know that your strength is that you do well one-on-one, you're typically a good listener, you're more at ease in structured environments, and you are more comfortable interacting around substance, rather than small talk. The key is to find ways to make connections and structure relationships around these strengths.

✓ If you're a student, try going through the alumni office to find connections rather than attending mixers or large job fairs. The alumni office can help you make more targeted connections that you can pursue one-on-one, which is typically easier for introverts.

✓ If you're a professional, try asking someone out for coffee one-on-one or start a correspondence with someone about a matter you're both interested in.

✓ Bring a wing woman! If you have to go to a larger event that you're nervous about, find a trusted friend or colleague who enjoys those types of activities to go with. She can help you start conversations with people and stop you from conversing solely with the buffet table all night.

Let's say you're excited and/or dreading the networking event you're attending tomorrow night. How do you prepare?

First, write down your goals for this event. Are you hoping to find a connection that will land you a job or a client or will help you get more information about a new field? Write down your top-three goals, so you can attend the event with a clear plan.

1. _____

_____

_____

2. _____

_____

_____

3. _____

_____

_____

Now, who are the target people you would like to meet? If you know who is going to be attending the event, write down their names. If you don't know, right down the type of person you have in mind, for example, entrepreneurs with companies in advertising, a marketing professional who can help you crack into the field, a fellow HR professional:

1. _____

_____

_____

2. _____

_____

_____

3. _____

_____

_____

Practice your elevator pitch. Your elevator pitch should be short, no more than three sentences, that clearly communicates who you are, why you've come, and your goals. For example:

I'm a plaintiff-side employment lawyer specializing in class actions for the past four years at X firm. I've really enjoyed X and Y aspects of my job, and I've been increasingly interested in how employment law and policy overlap. I'd like to get more experience drafting regulations and policies for workplaces.

Write down your elevator pitch:

_____

_____

_____

_____

_____

_____

What Should You Wear?

Ah, the eternal question. We are not going to tell you what to wear for two reasons: (1) because it can vary tremendously depending on what industry/event you're going to and (2) because we are not in the business of telling women how to present themselves. Especially for younger women, hearing people tell them what (not) to wear is exhausting and frustrating and can lead to endless fighting (just ask Marina's mom about when she was interviewing for colleges).

But we will say, we encourage you to dress in professional, culturally appropriate attire. What we mean by that is if you are interviewing for a job in academia at a traditional institution, a suit may be culturally appropriate. If you are attending a tech mixer where jeans and T-shirts are the norm in the workplace, a suit will be out of place. Our biggest piece of advice is to wear something you will be comfortable in. If you are comfortable and confident, you are more likely to make a good impression, regardless of what you wear. Obviously, there are some exceptions: probably don't wear something with lots of rips or tears, and make sure sensitive parts of your body are covered. Other than that, be authentic to who you are and think about the balance between wearing something comfortable for you and appropriate for the culture of the event.

Lastly, don't forget the details. These may seem small but can make the networking experience more comfortable:

✓ Wear something with pockets or bring a small bag to put business cards in. The last thing you want is to be wearing a cute, pocketless dress and have to clutch different business cards in your hand as you walk around.

✓ Eat before you go! Sometimes there is food at these events, but best case scenario, you'll probably get a couple of lukewarm appetizers. You don't want to be starving and slamming champagne while trying to impress.

✓ Don't bring a huge bag with you. It will be a pain to lug it around the whole time.

✓ Wear comfortable shoes. Specifically, wear comfortable shoes that *you are comfortable in*. If that means heels, great. If you're not super comfortable in heels, don't wear them! You want to feel confident and comfortable, and tottering around on unfamiliar stilts won't help you do that. Leave the slippers at home, but there are lots of options in the middle (flats, boots, etc.).

✓ Be conscious of the coat you wear. If it's winter, try to use the coat check or stash it somewhere at the beginning of the evening. If it's mild weather, wear a light coat that you can easily carry over your arm. It sounds small, but you don't want to be distracted or feel awkward lugging around bulky coats all evening.

✓ If you collect information in your phone, make sure you take the time either in the moment or later that night to put in some information that will help you identify the key aspects of the connection you just made. If you collect business cards, write down key information on the back of the card either later that night or, even better, periodically during the event. Make sure to include the following:

  ▷ Person's full name (Jane W. doesn't cut it two weeks later).

  ▷ Person's workplace.

  ▷ Person's area of interest or a topic of conversation that you both had in common.

  ▷ Any personal information you learned about the person: do they have kids/spouse/partner? do they enjoy hobbies or sports?

  ▷ Where you met the person (so important for following up later, especially if you go to lots of events).

  ▷ If you don't have a good memory for faces, make sure to Google the person afterward and save their picture in your phone. That way you can try and save yourself the awkwardness of reintroducing yourself to someone you already met. If you collected their business card, write down what they were wearing when you met. This can help jog your memory in the future.

Don't Forget the Follow-Up

Here's the part that takes some work: how you can turn a one-off conversation at a party into a meaningful network connection. Build following up into your work-life routine and make sure you find a system that works well for you.

First, who do you follow up with? Do you follow up with everyone whom you made a connection with, with everyone whose business card you collected? Maybe, but depending on how extroverted you are and how many people you talked to, it could be too many. One rule of thumb is to trust your gut. Was there someone whom you talked to that you clicked with? Did you talk to someone whom you genuinely enjoyed talking to, that you really liked? Often, these are the most fruitful connections that not only can end up helping you the most but can help you develop lasting and beneficial relationships. Networking isn't just about meeting people; it's about maintaining and growing your network as you move through different stages of your career. This will be much easier to do if you genuinely like the person you're connecting with.

Look over the connections you made at the event and come up with a prioritized list of whom you want to build a relationship with. List them here:

1. _____

2. _____

3. _____

4. _____

5. _____

6. _____

7. _____

DO! Follow up with people the day after the event.

DON'T! Get a business card from someone if you don't intend to follow up. That's a waste of everyone's time (unless politeness mandates that you accept it).

The next day, add the person on LinkedIn (If you missed it, read chapter 6 in the workbook for LinkedIn tips, tricks, dos, and don'ts). Make sure to write a personal message instead of the form message that LinkedIn gives you when you request to add someone to your network. Say something like, "Great to meet you last night at X. I'm sending you an e-mail. Would love to keep in touch."

Next, send the person an e-mail. Make sure to do the following:

1. Keep it short! No more than three lines.
2. Have a *specific, easy* ask. NOT: "I'd like to learn more about your organization." TRY: "I'd love to grab coffee" or "I'd love to have a fifteen-minute phone call to pick your brain about X."

If it's helpful, follow this form:

Dear_____,
    It was great to meet you at _____. I really enjoyed hearing about _____ and would love to discuss it further. I'd love to grab coffee and ask a couple of questions.

Notice that you didn't directly say, "When can you get coffee?" or even "Are you open to getting coffee with me?" At this point, when you're just testing the waters, you want to be as low maintenance as possible, and you want to write your correspondence in a way that lets both of you save face if it gets ignored. With this wording, your ask still comes across, but you put the person under no obligation to do anything.

Write out a sample e-mail you can send to someone you recently made a connection with:

_____

_____

_____

_____

_____

_____

How often do you bug somebody? What if you don't hear anything back? There are no single answers, but the basic rule of thumb is to . . .

Make It Substantive!

Even if you don't hear back from a contact you reached out to, you can still send them e-mails every once in a while (probably not more than one a month and not more than three every six months). But instead of e-mailing them variations on the same e-mail every time, find ways to connect substantively.

If you know the person is involved in a certain area or if they are known for work in a particular field or if you had a conversation when you met about a subject, send them related things that they might find of interest. If you read an article that's about their subject, send it to them with a note saying, "I read this and thought of you. Would love to hear your thoughts." Or if you're speaking on a panel about an issue they work on, invite them to it. Find ways to connect along lines of mutual substantive interest, rather than just "Hey, I want to know you!"

Note: When we say substantive, we don't mean serious. If you made a connection with someone over your mutual love of sea otters, you could send them an article about sea otters or a cute video, if it was appropriate.

One woman we know was trying to establish a connection with another woman, and they had a mutual love of shoes. So she subscribed herself to the Zappos e-mail list, and when she got a notice that Zappos was having a big sale, she forwarded it to her contact with a little note. This is a great example of connecting over substance, though not necessarily over matters of grave importance.

How do you keep track of all this following up and network building that you're doing? We have some tips:

✓ Set Google alerts: If you make a connection with someone, set up a Google alert with their name. That way, if they get a big promotion or get mentioned in an article, you'll know and be able to send a note via e-mail or LinkedIn congratulating them. In addition, if the person you made a connection with has a specific interest or area of expertise—say, tech mergers or work-life balance—set a Google alert with keywords that relate to that interest. Then, the next time Google buys a new app or Netflix introduces a great parental leave program, send that person a note saying, "I saw that X happened. Would love to get your take on it" or "I've been reading about X and thought of you. Great work getting this through!" This can go a long way to establishing a meaningful, substantive-based relationship with someone and can let them know you're not just interested in having them hire you in the future or donate money to your organization.

✓ Would this work with your connections? Think of a recent connection you made and a Google alert you could set up to help you keep in touch:

_____

_____

✓ Imagine that a Google alert came up around that topic or person. Draft a note that you would feel comfortable sending them:

_____

_____

_____

_____

_____

_____

✓ Set up calendar alerts. After making a connection with someone whom you'd like to develop a relationship with, set up alerts on your calendar for one week, one month, two months, and six months to follow up.

✓ Finally, it's good to keep an ongoing list of whom you want to keep in touch with and what you want to keep in touch about. It can look something like this:

Contact	Issue of mutual interest	Last time contacted	Next step	Notes
Liz Harrison	Investment banking / loves hiking	12/15—sent article about rising number of female investment banking professionals, with a note about hiking the Grand Tetons	Coffee scheduled! 2/24	Make sure to bring up recent legislation around offshore investment taxation rates

If you still do not hear back, move on. You're not going to catch every fish, and the connections you make should be mutual connections, not one-sided relationships.

If you *do* hear back, wonderful! Solidify a date and time to meet (in person is always best, but a call is better than nothing). Make sure to do your homework before your meeting or call. Look into the following:

✓ Background about the person you're meeting: any school connections, past work connections, whether they have been in the field for a long time or recently switched, any sticky/controversial areas to avoid:

_____

_____

_____

_____

_____

_____

✓ Recent events surrounding the topic you're interested in discussing: any big business deals, any news articles the person or their company were mentioned in, speeches they recently gave, recent publishings, and so on:

_____

_____

_____

_____

_____

_____

✓ Big actors/players in the topic you're discussing: if you act interested in a topic, you should be able to back it up. This is not to say you need to be an expert (that's why you're asking the person to meet, after all), but it's good to know the basics: who writes about this topic, what the big events were that led to the current state of the topic, what the major issues are on either side:

_____

_____

_____

_____

_____

_____

✓ Specific questions, asks, or offerings to the person you're meeting. Be ready with at least three *specific* questions for the person and at least one specific ask:

_____

_____

_____

_____

_____

There are ways to connect substantively with people other than drinking coffee. Here are some ideas:

1. Establish a book club and invite people you'd like to know better. It doesn't have to be about work-related books at all. You could read historical fiction or *Gossip Girl*. The point is to structure an interaction with a limited group of people around substantive issues.
2. Establish a club with people generally at your professional level that gets together and talks about leadership issues and career challenges.
3. Establish a Lean In circle and invite people who could be helpful to you professionally and/or could be helpful to have in your peer group.
4. Establish a mothers' group, hiking club, pickup soccer game, or the like—anything where you are interacting with people around issues of substance.

10

Getting the Most Out of Your Network

As we've discussed, networking isn't only about getting a job. Building and—just as important—maintaining your network can help your career no matter your employment status.

Joan is constantly building connections, reaching out to her network, and connecting different arms of her network. She uses her network to look for new board members or for lawyers to speak at our Leadership Academy, or she hears about someone who's doing really great work advancing women in the workplace and wants to explore collaboration possibilities. Other people use their networks to organize events they're putting on, to gather support for a new initiative, or to raise money.

What are some ways that your network could help you? Identify three goals you'd like to reach out to your network with:

1. _____
   _____
   _____

2. _____
   _____
   _____

3. _____
   _____
   _____

Do you already have someone in your network who could help you with each of these goals? If you do, write their names down here:

1. _____
2. _____
3. _____

If you don't already know people to help you with these goals, try to think of someone with whom your ask would be a mutually beneficial situation. For example, if you are organizing a panel on advertising in tech and need speakers, do you know anyone in the field who also needs clients? People who are more at the beginning stages of their careers and want to get their names out there tend to get more benefit out of speaking at events than people who are more established. Write down people you think might also benefit from your ask:

1. _____

_____

_____

2. _____

_____

_____

3. _____

_____

_____

This is a key tenet of maintaining your network: *make it a Win/Win*. Creating mutually beneficial relationships, where the other person gets something out of your continued connection, is the best way to ensure a long and fruitful relationship.

Remember the Zappos example? That was also an example of making it a Win/Win: for one woman, she solidifies her network contact. For the other, cheap shoes!

Here are some other ways to make it a Win/Win:

- ✓ Make sure you really do your homework about the person, so you know what they are interested in.
- ✓ Introduce the person to people you know that they would find interesting or helpful (this also puts you in the oh-so-important position of network broker).
- ✓ Find a niche that you can offer to people. One of our colleagues loves to travel, and when she gets back from a trip, she writes up a one-pager about the best places she stayed, hiked, ate, and so on. That way, when she hears that a contact in her network is traveling to Zion National Forest, she says, "Oh, I love Zion! I'll send you my recommendations."
- ✓ Offer to do favors for other people. If someone asks you to speak on a panel or introduce them to someone, do it! Even if you don't see the immediate gain in it for you, it will increase the economy of gratitude between you, and down the road it will probably pay off.

Essentially, the key to maintaining your network is to keep in touch with your contacts even when you don't need something. If every communication someone gets from you is asking them to do something, they are going to stop reading your e-mails. Make sure to send other types of communications: congratulations on a new job, happy birthdays, articles they might be interested in, and so on.

11

How Your Work Network Works

Over and over, when we work with organizations that are struggling with gender bias, the problem comes back to how their internal networks operate: white men talk to other white men, and then decisions get made. How are people hired? White men ask their friends who look like them if they know anyone for the job and—viola!—a white man gets hired for the job. And this doesn't just happen in the hiring process. When a marketing or PR company is about to land a big client, who knows about it first? Who gets picked to be on the team? When a law firm is considering promotions and partnership, who is talking to the people making the decisions?

There is often a big difference between the formal organizational chart in your workplace and the informal networks that run within it.[1] That's because not everything runs up formal organizational lines in exactly the way it should. How does information get passed around the office? Are there relationships between people that affect who get what opportunities? Is there someone around the office who, even though they may not be the head boss, everyone likes and respects and goes to with their problems?

_____

_____

_____

_____

_____

There are three types of informal organizational networks: the advice network, the trust network, and the communications network. Analyzing each of these networks in your workplace can help you strategically place yourself in a professionally beneficial position.

1. The Expertise Network

Whom do people in your office go to when they have a problem?[2] If you're working on a big case and you have a question about the best tactics for writing your brief, whom do you go to? Is there someone at the office who maybe isn't the most senior person but whom people rely on to have the expertise? Identify the person or a few people who are routinely called on for their expertise (maybe it's you!):

_____

_____

_____

_____

_____

_____

Where are you in relation to those people? Do you go to them for expert advice also? Are you one of the people your colleagues go to for advice?

_____

_____

_____

_____

_____

Now that you've identified the people at the center of the expertise network, consider bringing them into the fold when you want to start a new initiative or if you want to change a practice or policy around the office. Getting these people on your team will be essential to getting the whole workplace behind you.

How do you break into the expertise network if you're out of it? How do you raise your position? Think of ways you can demonstrate your expertise without yelling it from the rooftops. Maybe you could host a lunchtime panel on a specific issue and include yourself as one of the panelists. Or you could write up a one-pager on a new development in your field and send it around to everyone: "Just in case you found it useful, happy to answer any questions!" Write down some strategies that would fit in your workplace:

_____

_____

_____

_____

_____

If that doesn't work, consider trying to connect with someone who is influential in the expertise network along substantive lines. You could ask them out for coffee to discuss a specific topic. You could ask for their advice on a project you're working on that you know they would be interested in. How could this work in your organization?

_____

_____

_____

_____

_____

_____

2. The Trust Network

Whom do people in your office go to when they have a sensitive problem? Whom do they confide in? Whom do people trust to "have their back"? Maybe there is one person, or maybe every division has a person or two who fit this category. Identify the people you know who fit this description:

_____

_____

_____

_____

_____

Where are you in relation to those people? Are you one of them?

_____

_____

_____

_____

_____

_____

The trust network reveals the influencers in your organization. To be an effective leader in your workplace, you need to be a part of the trust network. A leader who is isolated from the trust network won't receive candid feedback from their staff, won't be trusted as much by their staff, and as such, won't receive the same level of loyalty and may actually cause employees to become defensive.[3]

If you're out of the trust loop, how can you reposition yourself? Identify a key player in the trust network whom you can form a relationship with. This might not be the top person or the most influential. If you're seriously out of the loop, try approaching someone who is in the middle of the trust network, someone you already have a connection with whom you trust. You could say, "I'd really love to get to know these people. Maybe I could join lunch sometime?" Is there someone at your workplace you trust whom you could talk to about this?

_____

_____

_____

_____

_____

_____

If not, is there someone in the trust network whom you'd like to form a connection with? Even if you don't know them at all, you can always ask them out to coffee and try to find common ground. Would that be possible at your job?

_____

_____

_____

_____

_____

_____

3. The Communications Network

Whom do people talk to? Who always seems to be in the know about work-related matters? Are there cliques at your workplace? Or is information more diffusely spread?

_____

_____

_____

_____

_____

_____

Where are you in the communications network? Do you know who's getting promoted before everyone else? Or do you feel shut out of the information flow?

_____

_____

_____

_____

_____

The communications network is essential to be aware of, especially for women. Often, the flow of information in a workplace stays in the boys' club, and sometimes it thrives in those after-hours happy hours that women are less likely to attend. (Note to Future Self: Another good reason to implement Wine Wednesdays: have happy hour at work so people can socialize and network without having to miss time with kids or sacrifice a life outside of work.)

What happens, then, is those lucky few in the boys' club know when there is a position opening before anyone else and can thus position themselves better for it. We've heard about companies announcing they've just landed a major client and in the same breath naming the (all-male) team they've assigned to it, before anyone else even had a chance to pitch. This is probably a result of an insular communications network. Can you think of a similar situation? What happened?

_____

_____

_____

_____

_____

If your workplace communications network is dominated by male cliques, there are strategies for dealing with this.

First, it's not all bad news. The cliques at your job are probably not as strong as they seem. Cliques are like echo chambers: they lack diversity of opinion, so they often miss out on crucial information. In addition, because cliques tend to be small, the ties between their members are very strong and thus very costly to maintain.[4]

If you're one of those women who fit in with the boys, who feel comfortable in close groups of men, keep making it work for you. If you're not, there's another option: become a network broker.

The key is creating ties with different people in your organization, people you maybe wouldn't ordinarily talk to and, importantly, people who probably don't know each other. Identify some potential people in your organization:

_____

_____

_____

_____

_____

These ties don't have to be strong ones. Try to find one thing to connect with someone about or a way to establish a small link so that if you wanted to ask them a question, you would feel comfortable contacting them. Think of a couple of ways to establish small connections with the people you identified above:

_____

_____

_____

_____

_____

It is incredibly beneficial to establish these weak ties to lots of different people in your organization. It can help your present work tremendously. For example, a female HR director told us she was having real trouble implementing a new diversity initiative that she had pioneered at her corporation. She had a few connections to people working in the legal department. She used those connections to get the legal department on board by explaining the strategic legal reasons behind her diversity initiative. With the legal department on board, the rest of the corporation was much more receptive to her initiative.

Furthermore, being a network broker can help your future career. Network brokers are more likely to get promoted than members of insular cliques are. Why? For one, having your toe in different networks allows you to hear about opportunities before other people. Also, having lots of weak ties to different networks means that your network is much larger than other people's, so it's more likely that you will "come to mind."[5]

Being a network broker can help you to sidestep the gender bias that exists within mostly male networks—networks that continue to dominate the business world. Because those networks are so insular and business is rapidly expanding its scope, when people in those networks need to connect to someone outside their clique, you will be in a unique position to broker that connection.

PART IV

Navigating Workplace Politics

12

Prove It (Over and Over) Again

Show It (Over and Over) Again

Think about it: if people are going to tend to remember your mistakes and overlook or discount your successes, you have to help them. 📖 (Read with "Strategy 1: Trump the Stereotype" on page 44 of *What Works*). Figuring out your metrics—and deploying them strategically—will help you highlight your successes and make it harder for people to hang on to your mistakes.

If What Matters Where You Work Is Clear

Some companies live and die by metrics; in those, this task will be straightforward. If you are in sales, your sales numbers probably matter a lot. If you are in academia, your publications and one or more citation indices do. Write below one to five metrics that matter where you work. (Typically, there will be only a few metrics that really matter, but if there are more where you work, feel free to list them!) The best way to show your value is by accumulating objective metrics that clearly demonstrate your value to your company.

1. _____

2. _____

3. _____

4. _____

5. _____

If What Matters Where You Work Is Far from Clear

In some workplaces, what matters is not so straightforward. If that's the case where you work, the first step is to identify objective metrics that matter at your company.

How can you find out what really matters? Work your network. Most useful are people right above your level to people one to five years ahead of you. How many of those people do you know well enough to ask, "I am trying to make sure I am doing what it takes to succeed here. What really matters? How can I develop objective ways of showing my contributions?" *If you don't know enough people to ask around effectively, you need to develop your network.* Refer back to part 3, "Networks," for strategies. Once you've done your homework, list metrics that matter where you work:

1. _____

2. _____

3. _____

4. _____

5. _____

Now that you've identified the numbers you are looking for, *put in the time necessary* to develop the data you need to show you've met the relevant metrics. It may seem like your time is better spent keeping your nose to the grindstone, but unless you can show people how much you've accomplished, your work might not get rewarded.

Congratulations! Now you have your metrics.

Accept Your Compliments Gracefully—and Write Them Down

(Read with "Strategy 1: Trump the Stereotype" on page 44 of *What Works*)

Remember in chapter 1 when we talked about taking compliments rather than deflecting them? The next step is to turn those compliments into building blocks for your career.

In your e-mail inbox, make a subfolder called "Personal Metrics" or "Smile File." Whenever you get a compliment in an e-mail, file it in that folder. No matter how big or small, anything in writing that shows you contributed value to a project or you added a new idea or did a good job, file it away.

If you get a great compliment in person, try to transfer it to writing. You could send the person an e-mail later saying, "Just wanted to thank you again for your positive feedback on the presentation I gave last week. It is helpful to my work going forward to know what works. Knowing that my preparation paid off and my presentation was successful is valuable to me."

Think of a recent time when you received a compliment in person. How could you have sent a follow-up e-mail that would have solidified the compliment in writing?

_____

_____

_____

_____

_____

If the person doesn't respond, it doesn't matter. File your e-mail away in your "Personal Metrics" folder. Keep filing away these compliments until you need them. They'll come in handy during performance evaluations (See chapter 14 in the workbook) or if you are negotiating salary (see chapter 8 in the workbook).

Steal Back Your Ideas

📖 (Read with pages 29–34 of *What Works*)

It happens again and again. A woman brings up a good idea, only to have it overlooked. Then a man repeats it, and now it's brilliant and all his. We call this the Stolen Idea. What's a girl to do?

Remember, as always, the three Ts: timing, tone, and tier. If you're just out of college, you can't call the CEO a turkey butt, but if you're the CEO, you might want to get straight to the point. (Note to Future Self: When you're the CEO and see someone taking credit for someone else's idea, call them a turkey butt. Things to consider: making a hat with a turkey butt on it and having them wear it? Maybe too much.)

Here are some smooth comebacks to help you counter the Stolen Idea by yourself:

- ✓ "Thanks for picking up on that idea. You've added something important. Here's the next step . . ."
- ✓ "Interesting you should say that. That's exactly the point I was making."
- ✓ "I think that's what I said. If you're disagreeing with me, I want to understand what you're saying."
- ✓ "Exactly. You understand what I'm thinking."
- ✓ "You may have been on your iPhone when I made that point."
- ✓ "You turkey butt. That was my idea."[1]

Of course, the most effective thing is for the women to band together with male allies and have the men consistently call it out whenever the Stolen Idea emerges. If a woman's idea is stolen, the ally simply says, "I've been thinking about that ever since Pam first said it. You've added something important. Here's the next step."

13

Are You Doing the Glamour Work or the Office Housework?

Women are expected to be nice, good team players, and not necessarily ambitious. That's why they so often find themselves doing large loads of office housework.

Some of this is literally housework. Picking up the room after a meeting, ordering lunch for the meeting, and planning parties—women seem to be expected to do these things far more often than men.

Other office housework is administrative work. Taking notes during the meeting, making sure to reserve a room, or getting people on the phone for a conference call are good examples.

A fourth kind of housework is "emotion work," the work of handling other people's emotions. Women professionals may be called on to act as the "office mother" or the "peacemaker," while men get a pass. Sometimes women professors are expected to mentor other people's students or to step in and help if a student is having difficulties—not only for their students but for their male colleagues' students, too.

The final kind of office housework is different. It's real work—it's just undervalued. If you ask women architects, "What's the office housework?" they'll tell you it's designing elevators and detailing bathrooms. Among surgeons, it's managing patient follow-up rather than spending time in the operating room. If you ask women litigators, they'll tell you it's doing the task list rather than arguing the motion in court. All over, women are more likely to do the PowerPoint than to be the ones who give the presentation to clients.

Here are the three basic strategies to address office housework issues. 📖 (Read with pages 110–116 of *What Works*.)

Strategy #1: Work behind the scenes to set up a rotation.
Strategy #2: Make the housework work for you.
Strategy #3: The strategic "no."

What's the office housework in your environment?

_____

_____

_____

_____

_____

What's the glamour work—the career-enhancing work?

_____

_____

_____

_____

Doing the office housework takes time away from more high-value work, and it may undercut your perceived competence for more highly valued work. But how do you get rid of large loads of office housework without being seen as "not a team player"? Studies show that women face higher expectations that they will engage in these "organizational citizenship behaviors," but they also typically get less credit for doing them.[1]

Do you do "office housework"? What kind(s)—literal housework, admin work, emotion work, important-but-devalued work?

_____

_____

_____

_____

_____

Do you feel women do more than their fair share? Note that sometimes it's a subgroup of women who carry the load. If you're not sure whether you're doing more than your fair share, it may help to do an assessment.

Examples of women doing literal housework or admin tasks:

1. _____

2. _____

3. _____

4. _____

5. _____

Examples of men doing literal housework or admin tasks:

1. _____

2. _____

3. _____

4. _____

5. _____

If there seems to be no real difference, that's great. Everybody's sharing these tasks pretty equally.

Another common pattern—an appropriate one—is when these less glorious tasks are shared by people who are at a relatively junior level. Is that the case where you work?

Examples of junior-level people doing literal housework or admin tasks:

1. _____

2. _____

3. _____

4. _____

5. _____

Examples of senior-level people doing literal housework or admin tasks:

1. _____

2. _____

3. _____

4. _____

5. _____

Examples of women doing emotion work:

1. _____

2. _____

3. _____

4. _____

5. _____

Examples of men doing emotion work:

1. _____

2. _____

3. _____

4. _____

5. _____

If women are stuck doing the housework, it's time to get proactive. Here are some basic strategies. Sometimes the hardest part is figuring out what's the proper forum in which to bring this up. Often, the first step is to talk with your mentor about what's the best strategy.

✓ If you are asked to do a housework or admin task, look around: is it always you who are asked? Always women? Always the rookies? If it's the rookies, then the best solution is to wait it out. If it's always you or always women, then—when asked—do it once, do it graciously, and then work behind the scenes to set up a rotation among a suitable group. You may want to enroll your network to help.

✓ If it's something that's actual housework, like planning parties or ordering lunch, then a good solution—if your company has admins—is to suggest that the admins do it, on the grounds that it will save time paying more expensive employees to do what is, after all, work that admins could probably do better.

✓ If it's admin work and your company does not have sufficient support staff to handle it, then the best approach is to set up a formal rotation.

If it's emotion work, things get more difficult. People often assume that women "are just better at stuff like that" and that "men aren't good at it." Here are a couple strategies that may help:

First, figure out if the emotion work that you're doing is helping you or hurting you. Sometimes you gain enough political capital by being the peacemaker that makes the emotional slog of emotion work worth it. Are you gaining anything by being the peacemaker?

_____

_____

_____

_____

_____

_____

What are you losing (time/energy/etc.) by being the office peacemaker?

_____

_____

_____

_____

_____

If you're losing more than you're gaining for doing the emotion work, one strategy is to try and work behind the scenes. Is there someone above you in your company whom you could go to and simply say, "This situation isn't working for me. What are our options?"

_____

_____

_____

_____

_____

If there's no one above you at your workplace who could help you, could you bring someone else in laterally to help? Maybe you could be only a part-time peacemaker? Think about the people who are in conflict: is there someone from a different department or from a different team who is familiar with the situation but not so involved?

_____

_____

_____

_____

_____

If the problem persists, and it's affecting your team, it might be time to find a more permanent solution. Could you transfer someone or wind up someone's workload and wind down someone else's?

_____

_____

_____

_____

_____

_____

Exercise

You have just been asked *again* to do an office housework task that is, in your view, not properly within your job description.

Use this list to jog your memory:

✓ Taking notes

✓ Cleaning up after a meeting

✓ Getting people on the line for a conference call

✓ Planning a party

✓ Mentoring junior colleagues

✓ Comforting a junior colleague who is upset or is having difficulties

Name three different ways you could work behind the scenes to make sure this doesn't happen again in the future.

1. _____

2. _____

3. _____

Think about ways that you could take an inconvenience (getting another task that you don't want) and use it to your advantage. If you're asked to plan a retirement party for a senior partner, ask that you work with someone close to the guest of honor, someone similarly high up in the company. Your stated reason can be wanting to throw the best, most personalized party possible, and the benefit will be establishing a connection and relationship with a higher-up.

Alternatively, you could use the new project as a way to trade away a project that's even worse. "Sure, I'll circulate the agenda for the meeting, but then I won't have time to get coffee and bagels. I'll ask Todd to do it."

Or just don't do it. Explain to the person giving you the project that in order to accommodate this new task, you would be jeopardizing other projects that are more important to the company. In most cases, your colleague will see that you have enough on your plate and back off.

Which is best? Explain your reasoning.

_____

_____

_____

_____

_____

_____

If you can't figure out which is best, describe how you will go about getting the information and advice you need to solve this problem.

_____

_____

_____

_____

_____

_____

Then there's the office housework that's real work—it's just undervalued. This varies a lot, but a common theme is that women do the backroom work, and men do the glamour work and get the glory (and the payoff for the women's backroom work!).

Examples of women doing less valued work:

1. _____

2. _____

3. _____

4. _____

5. _____

Examples of men doing less valued work:

1. _____

2. _____

3. _____

4. _____

5. _____

14

Getting Good Performance Evaluations and Getting Promoted

Self-Promotion

It's not really about asking for a raise, but knowing and having faith
that the system will give you the right raise. That might be one of
the initial "super powers," that quite frankly, women [who] don't ask
for a raise have. It's good karma. It will come back.
—Microsoft CEO Satya Nadella[1]

Carol Frohlinger calls it "the tiara syndrome": just keep your head down, do great work, and wait for someone to come and put a tiara on your head.[2]

Workplaces typically don't work like that, because men have been taught from a very young age that, if they want to get ahead, they will have to be competitive and ambitious. So men will be out there working the politics. Women who don't do so are often at a disadvantage.

Remember, other people are out there working the politics. You need to show your value and make sure other people know it. This is even more important for women than for men, because women often have to provide more evidence of competence than men do in order to be seen as equally competent. They have to prove themselves over and over again.

Using Your Metrics

📖 (Read with "Strategy 1: Trump the Stereotype" on page 44 of *What Works*)

We discussed in chapter 13 of the workbook how to figure out which metrics matter where you work, and we emphasized that it's important to take time to develop your own personal metrics. We also discussed what to do with compliments: write them down!

Now you need to let people know about it. Do people a favor: share your metrics, accomplishments, and compliments in usable form.

Reach out to your network—to your mentors and allies in the field, ideally who are higher up in your field. Ask them, "I got some great news today about a big project that I've been working on that I would love to share with you. What's the best way to keep you updated?"

Once you get the go-ahead, send updates to your mentors when you've hit a big goal, when you get a great compliment, or when you exceed your numbers for the quarter. It's up to you to make your competence visible. Think about it this way: you're saving time and trouble for people who want to help you. If your mentors want to advocate for you to get that plum assignment or promotion, you need to help them by making it easy for them to make the case that you're the one.

Identify several people in your network whom you could start sharing your metrics with:

1. _____

2. _____

3. _____

4. _____

5. _____

To help remind yourself, try setting a calendar alert for once every three months or however long makes sense for your position to send around an "update" e-mail to your mentors.

When you go in for your performance evaluation or to ask for a raise, bring your metrics (the ones that make you look really, extra awesome) and your "Smile File." That way, when the boss asks how you think you've done over the past year or asks why you should get the promotion, you can literally show them.

Communicating Your Value

Make sure you're communicating your value in your bio (or whatever document is more relevant in your environment).

First, let's talk about your bio. To write it, you will follow the same principles you followed in preparing a resume to get a job. An important principle is that most people need not one bio but a bio for each audience they seek to impress. For example, here's a bio for Angelina Jolie designed to land her a part in a film as a sex bomb:

Angelina Jolie is a world-famous and commercially successful actress and model. She has been named the "Sexiest Women Alive" by media outlets such as *Esquire*, *FHM*, *Empire*, and more. She has been voted "World's Most Beautiful Woman" by *Vanity Fair*. Her distinctive physical features have been written about in the *New York Times*, *Salon*, *Time* magazine, *Allure*, and the *New York Post*. Her trademark sex appeal and acting prowess led the *Lara Croft: Tomb Raider* movies to be some of the most commercially successful movies of her career.

Here's one designed to attract funds for a film she's seeking to direct:

Angelina Jolie has had one of the most successful film careers of all time. Spanning more than two decades, Jolie has acted in more than 30 films, which have collectively grossed more than *$2 billion* worldwide. Her films have been commercially and critically successful, reflecting Jolie's ability to select projects that appeal to broad audiences and tastes. As a producer, Jolie has distinguished herself further as a risk-taking and creative force. The projects she has produced have grossed almost $100 million worldwide. Jolie attracts top talent and tells unique stories that people want to hear.

Here's one designed to win her the lifetime achievement award from the Academy Awards:

By the time Angelina Jolie was 25 years old, she had starred in three major projects and won an Academy Award for her breakout performance in the 1999 drama *Girl, Interrupted*. She went on to solidify her leading actor status with high-octane features such as the *Lara Croft: Tomb Raider* series and *Mr. & Mrs. Smith*. In addition to her commercial success, Jolie has won significant critical acclaim for her work, resulting in two Screen Actors Guild Awards and three Golden Globe Awards. In the early 2010s, Jolie expanded her scope into directing, producing, and screenwriting and became a force for social change. Off-camera, Jolie has been leading the charge on international humanitarian and women's issues. She was named a UNHCR Goodwill Ambassador in 2001, has been on field missions to over 20 countries, and became the first recipient of the Citizen of the World Award.

Notice how she's used objective metrics to demonstrate her accomplishments. She's not bragging; she's just giving facts. Take your 250-word bio (or create one), or if a different document is more relevant in your environment, take that instead. Rewrite it, inserting your objective metrics and making sure you put your best foot forward in every way. Also be sure to add awards and other honors if they aren't there already.

To get you started, write the top-five things you want people to remember from your bio here:

1. _____

2. _____

3. _____

4. _____

5. _____

Now rewrite your basic bio.

How many bios do you need? What are the different audiences they are designed to impress?

_____

_____

_____

_____

_____

Adapt your bio for each audience. We'll assume you have three different bios. You've completed your first. Now do two more.

Second bio. Audience: _____. Bio:

_____

_____

_____

_____

_____

What are the key facts you identified that are most likely to impress this audience?

1. _____

_____

2. _____

_____

3. _____

_____

4. _____

_____

5. _____

_____

Third bio. Audience:_____. Bio:

_____

_____

_____

_____

_____

_____

What are the key facts you identified that are most likely to impress this audience?

1. _____

_____

2. _____

_____

3. _____

_____

4. _____

_____

5. _____

_____

Make Sure You're Using All Available Tools to Communicate Your Value
📖 (Read with "Strategy 1: Trump the Stereotype" on page 44 of *What Works*)

What are other tools available to communicate your potential and your achievements? Here are some ideas:

✓ If your office has a website, make sure your bio section is comprehensive, is up-to-date, and lists your degrees, scholastic achievements, and professional successes.

✓ If your office has a public calendar, don't hesitate to put important appointments up so that other people will know you're in demand.

What are other tools in your environment? List some here:

1. _____

2. _____

3. _____

4. _____

5. _____

Would You Like to Play a Specialized or Technical Role?

(Read with pages 53–56 of *What Works*)

If you feel like your path to promotion is blocked for some reason, one strategy that sometimes works is to seek a specialized or technical role. For example, if you are in a role in finance where all that matters are certain metrics—how much money you bring into the firm—then you might find various forms of bias less of an issue.

In addition, some women find that if they develop a valuable specialty, that's a ticket to success because they are consulted as experts, so to speak, rather than as women colleagues who are being judged by the same metrics and so present more of a threat.

A third situation where playing a technical role may help counter Prove-It-Again! problems is in an industry, such as tech, where those who play technical roles are seen as adding the most value. Women coders in tech persistently report that, when they move into management roles, people seem to instantly forget that they have technical skills—and that this doesn't happen to the men (who are often seen as highly competent individuals who are "taking one for the team" by agreeing to play a management role).

This may not be the path for you, but it's worth thinking about whether it is.

What are the technical roles for which you are qualified that are relevant in your environment?

_____

_____

_____

_____

_____

_____

Do those roles appeal to you?

_____

_____

_____

_____

_____

_____

What would you give up if you stuck to a technical or specialized role?

_____

_____

_____

_____

_____

_____

What would be the advantages of doing so?

_____

_____

_____

_____

_____

_____

15

Is There a Tug of War On?

📖 (Read with pages 179–218 of *What Works*)

Is there a Tug of War at your workplace? As we discussed in the introduction, Tug of War happens when gender bias in the environment plays out between women. Sometimes there is only one "woman's spot" on a committee or on a leadership team, which creates a dynamic where women have to fight each other to get the spot. Other times there is intergenerational conflict between women: younger women think that the older women in their office are too hard on them; older women think younger women "just don't get it." Sometimes women distance themselves from other women in the office, which creates resentment. Sometimes women are labeled "Queen Bees" or "Mean Girls."

It is important to recognize that the problem usually isn't women; the problem is the conditions that women have to deal with every day. The problem is gender bias, and sometimes gender bias ends up playing out between women. Notions of "sisterhood" and "women stick together" are good, but sometimes it doesn't happen that way. This chapter addresses what to do if you're having trouble with women in your office. Our approach asks you to think through why you may be having trouble with women in your office, considering all the ways that gender bias can pit women against each other.

First, are you having trouble with women in your office? If you're not, it may be worthwhile to still skim through the chapter. If you are, is it one woman in particular, or do you feel like you don't fit in with the other women you work with?

_____

_____

_____

_____

_____

_____

Tokenism

📖 (Read with pages 182–184 of *What Works*)

Sometimes conflict is created between women at your work because there is known to be only one "woman's spot" up for grabs. This spot could be for a high-level committee, on a board, or the like. Is this what's happening at your work?

_____

_____

If it is, the first step would be to figure out if there is a way to change it. Perhaps you could organize a meeting with the women who are competing for the spot and try to strategize together to open up more opportunities. This not only helps create more opportunities for women but may help to foster a better working relationship among the women in your office. Would this be possible where you work? Why or why not?

_____

_____

_____

_____

_____

_____

If opening up more spots for women at your office isn't an option, would it be possible to work out a system to share the position? If it's a committee position or a chance to lead a project, what about proposing that each person fills the role for a year and then passes it to the next person? Would that work with your situation? Why or why not?

_____

_____

_____

_____

_____

_____

If there's no solving the problem and if your career development depends on you getting that one "woman's spot," it might be time for you to consider transition to a workplace where there are more opportunities for women to advance. Go to part 7, "Leave or Stay?"

Strategic Distancing

Sometimes women who face gender bias respond to it by positioning themselves with the in-group and distancing themselves from the out-group (women). Yahoo CEO Marissa Mayer explained, "I'm not a girl at Google. I'm a geek at Google."[1] We call this strategic distancing. Or if you'd prefer the less technical name, "Why would I want to hang out with those losers anyway?"

Do you know this woman in your workplace? Is it you?

_____

_____

_____

_____

_____

This strategy makes sense for some women; certainly it did for Marissa. After all, men aren't expected to support other men all the time. There may be limits to notions of sisterhood, and that may be okay.

If you're strategically distancing yourself from other women and it's working for you, keep doing what works. One potential drawback to watch out for is your network. Make sure you have people that can support you professionally when you're having a hard time and need to talk to someone you can trust. For more, see part 3, "Networks."

Sometimes gender bias is so pervasive in a workplace that it hurts women to align with other women or even to associate themselves with women. We call this the *loyalty tax.* "I know she didn't *like* the things that were going on but she accepted them and refused to stand up in any way or even admit, publicly, there was a problem."[2] Are you noticing other women strategically distancing themselves at work? Is it affecting you?

_____

_____

_____

_____

_____

It may be annoying, but remember that she's probably acting that way as a response to the gender bias that she has faced over her career.

One solution may be to try to connect with the woman substantively, over work-related matters. If she's strategically distancing herself, she probably won't be interested in joining the women's book club or even engaging in social office activities with other women. But asking for her technical expertise on a project (or offering yours) could be a way to establish a connection and ease the tension. Could you try this at your workplace?

_____

_____

_____

_____

_____

For Younger Women

📖 (Read with pages 210–212 of *What Works*)

If you're a younger woman who is having trouble with a senior woman because you feel like she's too hard on you, consider what it took for her to get the position that she's in. She probably has been having to prove herself, over and over again, for decades, in a workforce that was even more resistant to women than it is today.

Do you know what it has taken for her to get where she is now? Does any of it sound familiar to what you have faced?

_____

_____

_____

_____

_____

If you don't know about her past, a great icebreaker would be to ask the woman about it. Consider inviting her out to coffee or lunch and asking about her early career. How has she managed to navigate through gender bias?

_____

_____

_____

_____

_____

_____

It's important to remember that, as younger women, we may have it a little easier. This is not saying that what we go through isn't difficult, trying, and unfair. But there is a precedent for it. Senior women today were often the only women in their class, the only women on the floor; they were the exception to the rule. And they had to adapt to those hostile conditions the best they could. For a lot of senior women, this meant being better than everyone else, never showing weakness, staying late and arriving early. As such, they may subconsciously (or consciously) hold you to those same standards. They probably aren't trying to be mean; they are more likely just reflecting the strategies that worked for them.

If that sounds familiar or fits your situation, have you ever said "thank you"? A simple thank-you to a senior woman in your life can go a long way. And it doesn't cost you anything. Could you offer a thank-you to the woman you're having a problem with?

_____

_____

_____

_____

_____

_____

In addition, try writing out a couple of lines about how the senior woman's experience was different from yours. If there are aspects that are easier today for you than they were for her, it may help to revisit them when you're feeling especially frustrated.

_____

_____

_____

_____

_____

_____

Relatedly, sometimes younger women get frustrated because they feel like the senior women in their office aren't helping them. This is a common situation we hear about. "She knows what it's like. Why isn't she helping to make this easier for other women?"

Our first response to this question is, are you sure she can? Just because she is a more senior woman, it may not mean that she has a lot of political capital to throw around. We've seen how women, on all steps of the ladder, can still be forced to walk a tightrope, to prove themselves over and over again, to sacrifice their personal lives so they are viewed as equally competent to the men. Maybe the senior woman isn't offering to help because she isn't in a position to. Do you think this is what's going on?

_____

_____

_____

_____

_____

_____

_____

If it is, she may be having just as hard a time as you, just in a different position.

For Senior Women

📖 (Read with pages 208–210 of *What Works*)

Your workplace probably looks very different than it did when you first started. When Joan first started working, she was one of only a few women, and women had to be at the far end of the continuum to make it in the workplace. They had to assimilate to an environment that was hostile toward them and had to be comfortable displaying "masculine assertiveness" to be heard.[3] Lots of senior women in the workplace today fit in when they were starting out by embracing their masculine side, sacrificing for their careers, staying late, and never taking vacations.

Today, you may look around your workplace and see younger women who project feminine personas, who take months or even years off to take care of their family, who want to work 40 hours a week with a flexible schedule and still get promoted. Do you find yourself passing judgments on the younger women in your office?

_____

_____

_____

_____

_____

_____

If you do, consider where you were when you were starting out in the workplace. Do you wish you could have shown your feminine side more or taken more time off to raise your kids?

_____

_____

_____

_____

_____

If that rings true, give yourself a pat on the back. Things are getting easier for the next generation of women. The workplace is becoming a less hostile environment. If you have kids, your daughter will be able to pursue her career dreams without totally sacrificing her personal life. Try listing out a few ways that the next generation having it easier will positively affect you and your family:

_____

_____

_____

_____

_____

If that doesn't assuage your concerns, you're not alone. We hear from senior women that they are concerned about the younger generation of women in the workplace: they're never going to make it! Remember that this is a sign of *success*: women don't have to fit into (as small) boxes anymore.

"She's a Bad Mother!" "She's a Bad Worker!"

📖 (Read with pages 198–203 of *What Works*)

Regardless of where you are on the seniority spectrum, you probably encounter women who are very different from you, who have very different ideas of what it means to be a "good woman" or a "good mother" or a "good worker." Some of your colleagues might act very differently from you, might make different choices than you would. Sometimes you may not understand the choices they make. Is there someone in your workplace who does motherhood really differently than you did?

_____

_____

_____

_____

_____

_____

Is there someone at your workplace who has a totally different approach to her work than you do?

_____

_____

_____

_____

_____

_____

These differences can sometimes trigger crises of confidence within ourselves, so it's important to be aware of what's at stake before passing judgment on someone else—or on yourself. Just because you could only take two weeks off when your son was born and your colleague took two months doesn't mean you're a bad mother. Just the same, just because someone comes in at seven a.m. every day and you come in at nine a.m. after you drop your kids off at school doesn't mean you're a bad worker. (Note to Future Self: Don't care about when people work or when they don't. Just focus on if the work gets done or not. Also, consider enforcing a strict "no work before nine a.m. rule" because really that would benefit everyone, right?)

Resist the urge to turn someone else's differing choices into a judgment about yourself. The norms of the "ideal worker" and the "ideal mother" don't work in today's society, yet they continue to weigh on us all. The more we can shrug off those pressures, while pursuing our goals, the more we advance the workplace for the next generation.

At the end of the day, more women in the workplace means more opportunities for us all. Make yourself a mantra: "all women are different" or "all mothers are different." Write it out here:

_____

_____

_____

_____

_____

You don't have to click with every woman in your office. You don't even have to like them. But every woman has to make these difficult choices about how to succeed in a workplace that is usually still dominated by men. We all make our own choices about how to do this, and sometimes they rub us the wrong way.

If you're someone who feels it's important to uplift and support other women, we thank you for it. See "Five Ways to Support Other Women" on page 216 of *What Works*.

If you're not, we get that too. We just hope you'll think twice before going out of your way to *undermine* another woman. Because that's not helping anyone.

16

Holding Your Own in Meetings and Getting Your Due for Teamwork

Often meetings are important. Reputations for brilliance stem from brainstorming sessions—and you can't get a word in edgewise. Women in meetings face both Prove-It-Again! and Tightrope problems.

Remember that brilliant physicist (or entrepreneur or . . . you name it)? You don't fit the mold. So people aren't primed to expect a brilliant idea from you, which means they might not notice it when it's offered.

Particularly if your work culture encourages people to act like an Alpha Dog, women may be at a disadvantage if they get judged when they act as assertive as the men act.

So you may find yourself walking a Tightrope. Be yourself, and you can't get a word in. Try to assert yourself, and you may get treated like a prima donna.

A closely related issue is how you can get your due for team work. This chapter addresses that, too.

"People Tell Me I Don't Command the Room"

If you're having trouble being heard, the first step is to do a reality check. Discuss the matter with one of your mentors and allies who has seen you in action. Choose one to whom you can show vulnerability. Some people don't respect people who display vulnerability; they do bravery or bravado and only respect that. Don't go to them. Go to someone in your network who has shown an interest in your career and say you'd like 15 minutes to talk in order to enhance your effectiveness at work, at a time convenient to them. Only 15 minutes.

When the meeting starts, don't spill out every iota of your free-floating anxiety. Say something like, "I'm doing a reality check because sometimes I don't feel I'm really able to get my points across effectively. Is it your perception that I command authority? It's something I've been thinking about." See what they say.

If you hear from someone you trust that you "lack executive presence" or "don't command the room," then go back to chapter 2, "Overcoming Your Own Tightrope Bias."

You're on the Tightrope here. People who don't express confidence and authority are seen as, well, nonauthoritative. For men, the solution is simple: act authoritative. For women, it is less simple, alas. Research shows that displays of confidence, directness, and authority can actually *decrease* women's influence but *increase* men's.[1] (Note to Future Self: Must figure out how to change this.) Why? Prescriptive stereotypes again. Women are supposed to be modest and self-effacing.

If you feel this playing out at work, you have three choices.

1. **Be direct and authoritative, and damn the consequences. Maybe it will work.**

2. **Decide that this is $&#%$ and that you don't want to work in that environment.**

3. **Use gender judo.**

I hate to tell you this, girl, but research shows that tentative language and a warm, co-operative style increase women's influence.[2] So the strategy is to do a masculine thing—make your point—but in a feminine way. Before you embrace this strategy, make sure that you're solving the right problem—that you're being perceived as too timid. If you're being perceived as too direct and authoritative, then obviously the fix will be different.

Does this feel comfortable to you? We would advocate showing warmth and communality rather than using tentative language, although in situations where you have authoritativeness to spare, the latter can be a good move, too—but only if you have authoritativeness to spare.

Did you try it? Did it work?

_____

_____

_____

_____

_____

_____

"I Can't Get a Word in Edgewise!"

Have you ever been in a meeting where the men are talking nonstop, talking over each other, and interrupting a lot, and you feel like you can't get a word in edgewise? Have you ever tried to do just as the men do—interrupt someone, talk over people—and felt a slight chill in the air, as if you just did something inappropriate?

When women are in groups that include both men and women, they tend to interrupt less, make fewer task suggestions ("We should do this"), and use tentative forms of speech ("Don't you think?"). The "I wonder ifs" disappear in women-only groups.

The next time you are in a meeting, do this exercise. Count how many times the men interrupt the women. Then count how many times the women interrupt the men.

Men interrupting women:

_____

Women interrupting men:

_____

Is there a problem? Are women getting interrupted more than men? If so, it's time to take action.

The first step is to learn how to "step on the end of a sentence." One woman's mentor told her to wait until it seems like the man talking is powering down and then begin talking. If he stops, you're there. If he doesn't stop, say, "I'm so sorry. I thought you were done." That's gender judo, a way of claiming the floor without violating people's sense of what kind of behavior is "appropriate" in a woman.

Try "stepping on the end of a sentence." How did it go?

_____

_____

_____

_____

_____

_____

"They Interrupt Me but Not Each Other"

Men interrupt more, participate more, and get more encouragement to do so.[3] Women are less likely to interrupt, are less likely than men to gain the floor when they do, and typically are offered fewer chances to participate.[4] (Note to Future Self: Consider using turkey butt hat for people who interrupt, also.)

Ben Barres, a Stanford neurobiologist who is a trans-man, told Joan in an interview, "By far, the biggest difference is that people treat me with far more respect. I can even complete a whole sentence without being interrupted by a man."

Why do men feel they can interrupt? They're under gender pressures themselves, of course, to show that they're men to be reckoned with. So they jump in. But—back to prescriptive stereotypes—when women interrupt, that may feel jarring: where's that modest, self-effacing team player?

The best way to handle this is to point it out to an ally, preferably male. "I know people are probably not aware they're doing this, but I feel like I'm interrupted a lot more than the guys are. In fact, I've kept track, and I am. Any chance you could keep an eye out for that for the next few meetings and just say something like, 'Amy, I think you had a thought there?'"

Might this work? Whom could you enlist to help? Keep in mind that the interruption problem also affects other groups, notably people of color and introverts—including introverted men. You could offer to help them in return.

_____

_____

_____

_____

_____

_____

    Another approach is to make sure you run the meeting and then set up certain protocols. Here are some possibilities:

- ✓ Establish norms: we work for even distribution of turns.
- ✓ Establish and enforce "no interrupting rule."
- ✓ Assign people to speak/report on specific issues.
- ✓ Allow people to contribute after the meeting.
- ✓ Circulate the agenda beforehand.

Again, all of these will help introverts, male or female. Could you talk with the person running the meeting and suggest one or some of these? If so, which one(s)?

_____

_____

_____

_____

_____

    Did anything get implemented? If so, did it work to establish a more even distribution of turns?

_____

_____

_____

_____

_____

_____

"Other People Get Credit for Ideas I Originally Offered"

Ah, the Stolen Idea again. Use the same strategy as for being interrupted (also refer back to the strategies in chapter 12, "Prove It (Over and Over) Again").

Find an ally. It may be someone else you see it happening to or a colleague who's a good person and might like to help you.

Whom could you enlist to help?

_____

_____

_____

_____

_____

_____

Again, the alternative is to ask a male ally or senior woman. "I know this is largely unconscious, but I feel like other people often get credit for ideas I originally offered. Would you feel comfortable speaking up when this happens?"

Did the person you asked to help agree to do so? Did they manage to help?

_____

_____

_____

_____

_____

_____

If you feel like the Stolen Idea's a big issue for you, it may be because you aren't being forceful enough. "I just keep asking questions and lead them to the answer, rather than stating it straight out," one woman told us. She was using gender judo, because her sense was that if she just did what the guys did—"we should do this"—it would not be well received. But note how easy it is to discount your contribution if you take the "lead them to water" approach. If the stolen idea's a big problem, try being a lot more direct, with a lot of warmth and signaling that your goal is to help the team. At least then you'll have a different problem!

"I'm an Expert, but No One Listens to Me!"

This is a dangerous situation—for you and for them. We once talked with a woman scientist who got such grief every time she said "No, that won't work" that she told us, "I brought up a mistake in their analysis, and when I argued for my point, I was labeled aggressive. Now I'm just bringing in baked goods and being agreeable."

We advise against this, because to do so means you are not doing your job and can legitimately be written up for poor performance. If that's the only option, it's time to leave, quick. Read part 7, "Leave or Stay?" One study showed that women were *less* influential when they possessed expertise, whereas men were—you guessed it—*more* influential. As a result, teams with a female expert underperformed compared to groups with male experts, for the simple reason that the female experts' opinions were less likely to be listened to.[5]

If this happens, you can take one of two tacks:

1. Go it alone. "Hey, folks, next meeting I'd like to set aside twenty minutes to familiarize you with the research base I'm working from."
2. Enlist help. "Hey, I need people to focus on this. May I have twenty minutes the next meeting to present the research that suggests a different direction?"

Would either of these work for you? Which one? If it's the second, whom would you enlist to help?

_____

_____

_____

_____

_____

_____

Did it work? If so, great. If not, what's the next step you will take to get people to listen to you? Keep trying. Remember, if you're being paid to bring your knowledge to bear, you need to find some way to do that—or to leave.

_____

_____

_____

_____

_____

_____

"I Feel Like I Don't Get the Credit I Deserve"

This issue is closely related to the Stolen Idea. When work is performed in groups, women tend to be rated as less competent, less influential, and less likely to have played a leadership role. Also, women tend to give more credit to male team members and are less likely to take credit unless their contribution was irrefutably clear.[6]

Do you feel this has happened to you?

_____

_____

_____

_____

_____

If it has, you need to make sure people know your contributions. How could you document your contributions in a way that does not feel too confrontational? Often the best way will be to think up a way to highlight your contributions in the frame of "I'm telling you this information to help you do something you've been tasked with." Gender judo again: "what a helpful person" (aka good woman).

Might this work for you?

_____

_____

_____

_____

_____

If not, is there another gender judo move you could make? Here are some ideas to jog your memory:

1. "I'm giving you information to help you."
2. Give the information with warmth.
3. "I'm giving you the information to help ensure the success of the team we're both on."
4. Have a sponsor, mentor, or ally give the information.

Might any of these work for you? Which one?

_____

_____

_____

_____

_____

_____

"How Do I Express Disagreement without Being Seen as a Bitch?"

Disagreement over values and personality conflicts, not surprisingly, corrode team performance.[7] But disagreements about how best to do the task at hand, if civil, can enhance team performance. Of course, you need to be mindful not to spend any more political capital than you have.

Is the disagreement you have about values or personalities or about how best to perform a task?

_____

_____

_____

_____

_____

_____

If you find yourself in a persistent conflict with someone who's undercutting you, reread pages 214–217 of *What Works* for an awesome way to cut short that kind of behavior.

If the disagreement is about the task, present the disagreement as your attempt to be a good team player and ensure the success of the group.

Did that work?

_____

_____

_____

_____

_____

_____

_____

_____

Of course, that's gender judo again. Good luck with your teams and meetings!

17

Okay, It's Not All in Your Head

The Maternal Wall is not all in your head. Maternal Wall bias is very real. In fact, it's by far the strongest form of gender bias.[1]

Motherhood can trigger very strong assumptions that a woman is no longer committed to her career or even competent at it. Thus, many mothers find they have to prove themselves all over again after they return from maternity leave—it's Prove-It-Again! squared.

If you are a mother, did you find yourself faced with any of these assumptions after you had children?

_____

_____

_____

_____

_____

_____

If the people around you seem to assume that you're no longer as committed now that you're a mother, how can you signal to them that you remain committed? This can be as simple as putting a sign on your office or cubicle telling people where you are when you're out at a business meeting (to counter the assumption that you are home with your kids). What are some simple things like that you can do?

_____

_____

_____

_____

_____

_____

Another really effective way to counter the automatic assumption that a mother is no longer as committed to her career is to signal that you remain career focused. Usually the best way is to ask a key person in your environment (either the person making the inaccurate assumption or someone who can help you advance) for a meeting and then tell them your ambitions for the next year and the next five years and ask them for advice about what steps you should take in order to achieve your goals. This also will ensure that the person doesn't "do you a favor" and withhold opportunities because "she has a lot on her hands right now." Do you think you could do that? Whom would you ask?

_____

_____

_____

_____

_____

_____

Make sure you check back periodically with this person, reporting on what you have done and asking what are the next steps.

Okay, now you try it. How did it go?

_____

_____

_____

_____

_____

In addition to mothers encountering assumptions that they *won't* remain committed or competent, some mothers meet assumptions that they *shouldn't* remain committed or work long hours. "I don't know how you can leave your kids so much; my wife would never do that"—comments like that. Have you encountered any similar comments?

_____

_____

_____

_____

_____

If you meet these kinds of comments, typically the best approach is to smile sweetly and say something like, "Well, I'm sure that's right for your family, but I'm doing what's right for mine: happy families are not all alike." Do you think you could do that? Remember to keep your tone light—and smile. The person made a jerky remark, but perhaps they meant well, and even if they didn't, it's not worth spending your political capital on (the men sure aren't).

Okay, now try it. How did it go?

_____

_____

_____

_____

_____

_____

Transitioning onto and off of Maternity Leave

One thing that's super important is to try to make sure that you transition your work when you go on maternity leave so that no one gets left, baffled, holding the bag. Your employer should have a formal system for this, but if that's not in place, you can just do it yourself. And remember, babies often come early—Joan had someone go out on maternity leave six weeks earlier than anticipated. Joan was extremely grateful for the detailed transition memo her employee left so that the temporary replacement knew exactly what was left hanging and whom to contact to pick up the thread.

If you are pregnant, who is the right person to go to in order to set up a transition plan? This may be your direct supervisor or the head of your group. Ask for an appointment when you are about two months from your delivery date and discuss a transition plan.

If you're pregnant, try it and write here how it went:

_____

_____

_____

_____

_____

_____

Pregnant women also should discuss before they leave how they are going to transition back into work. Maybe you can pin things down now; if not, then at least set up a procedure to follow once you return to work, such as, "Let's meet my first day back, and we can decide what work I will pick up." Remember, *you do not have to do this during your leave, and it is illegal (assuming the Family and Medical Leave Act applies) to ask you to do work during your maternity leave.* Go to human resources if that becomes a problem.

What If You Decide to Work Part-Time, Telecommute, or Request a Flex Schedule?

Sad to say, flex schedules are often stigmatized (although this may be litigable sex discrimination). If you decide to work a flex schedule, you have to be particularly careful to signal that you are still committed and that you still want good work.

How do you decide whether you want a flex schedule? First read chapter 19, "Negotiating Work-Family Conflict," and make sure your partner is pulling their weight at home. Don't assume it's you who has to cut back on work—that leaves you in a weak bargaining position. If you and your partner decide it's you who has to cut back, make sure you get the support you need to keep growing your career. A common pattern is for the partner who continues to work full-time to assume that the family has agreed that they no longer have significant caregiving responsibilities if they conflict with their career—or at all.

How do you ask for part-time or a flex schedule? The same way you do for anything else: make the business case, describing exactly how it would work, how the work of the department can still get done, and how your proposal will benefit the department. Prepare for this as you would for any other business meeting, and keep the "oh my God if you don't give me this I will just die, I am so overwhelmed" out of it. Use this space to begin sketching out your proposal:

_____

_____

_____

_____

_____

_____

_____

_____

_____

_____

_____

Now do a dry run of the meeting with your partner or a friend. Did that help? Don't have the conversation at work until you feel calm and confident that what you are offering will work out well for everyone involved.

And make sure you are around for high-profile events or key times that are critical for bonding. What are these in your workplace?

_____

_____

_____

_____

_____

_____

Now go bargain with your partner to make sure you can attend them.

Also, use the same strategies to counter the flexibility stigma that you used when you returned from maternity leave: leave a note on your office or e-mail when you are unavailable due to a business meeting (so people don't assume you are with your kids), have a meeting with your supervisor or sponsor to discuss your short- and long-term career plans, and so on.

PART V

Handling Difficult Conversations Successfully

(Hint: First step: don't avoid them like the plague.)

We've all been there. Your performance evaluation was lower than you think was justified. You get a surge of anger when you see that your partner left the seat up *again*. You mother keeps making little digs you think are just so unfair.

It's time for a difficult conversation.

First step: Don't run for the hills and then volcano with anger when you can't control your frustration any longer. That's the way many of us were brought up to handle difficult conversations. Joan should know—she was one of them.

Luckily, thanks to the path-breaking work of the Harvard Negotiation Project, there's now a formula for handling difficult conversations. We urge you to buy the book *Difficult Conversations: How to Discuss What Matters Most*, by Douglas Stone, Bruce Patton, and Sheila Heen. Read the whole thing.

What's so great about *Difficult Conversations* is that the authors decode the structure of difficult conversations and reveal that although conversations may seem different on the surface, they actually all share a common structure. Once you learn the structure, you can apply to it any and every difficult conversation in your life. From the authors:

In studying hundreds of conversations of every kind we have discovered that there is an underlying structure to what's going on, and understanding this structure, in itself, is a powerful first step in improving how we deal with these conversations. It turns out that no matter what the subject, our thoughts and feelings fall into the same three categories, or "conversations." And in each of these conversations we make predictable errors that distort our thoughts and feelings, and get us into trouble.[1]

What we present here is a supplement designed to help you take the important learning from that book and apply it to your own life, at work and at home.

18

Difficult Conversations at Work

We've all had them. Conversations you dread and rehearse over and over ahead of time, searching for some magic phrasing to make a tough message go down easy. A difficult conversation is anything you find hard to talk about, whether a low-stakes everyday interaction (asking your colleague across the hall to close the door when he's on the phone) or a high-stakes conversation (asking for a raise or giving a critical performance evaluation).

What's the last difficult conversation you had at work?

_____

_____

_____

_____

_____

Were you satisfied with the result? How did you feel afterward? Did you get your desired outcome?

_____

_____

_____

_____

_____

_____

The Difficult Conversations Model

Difficult conversations are complicated. Most contain three layers of conversation:[1]

1. The "What Happened" Conversation

On the surface, the parties disagree on the facts—what happened or should've happened and who's to blame. Often people have different perceptions of the situation. For example:

In a difficult conversation between Jane (supervisor) and Kate (subordinate), Jane is upset because Kate failed to turn in an assignment on time. Jane's view of the facts is she gave Kate a clear deadline and stressed this was a high-priority assignment, yet Kate failed to properly manage her time and missed the deadline.

Kate perceives the facts quite differently. She recalls Jane being vague about the deadline and failing to communicate the urgency of the assignment. Given Kate's heavy workload and pressing assignments for other supervisors, she thought her other assignments took priority. Kate worked several late nights to get everything done (including Jane's assignment) and thought she did a good job juggling it all.

Jane didn't know Kate had important assignments from other supervisors. Kate didn't know that Jane needed her assignment in order to prepare a presentation for a major client.

2. The Feelings Conversation

Difficult conversations also involve emotions. Each party brings feelings into the conversation that sometimes go unaddressed yet loom like an elephant in the room. Often people assume the best way to have a difficult conversation is to keep feelings out of it. This is not realistic. If it's difficult, you probably have feelings about the topic—and so does the other person.

Going back to the example above:

Jane feels frustrated about her inability to rely on Kate.

Kate feels like she's spinning her wheels working on assignments for different people and yet no one appreciates her.

3. The Identity Conversation

Difficult conversations raise the question "What does this situation say about me?" Often a conversation becomes difficult when one or both parties' identities are put at risk. "Is he really saying that I'm stupid?" "That I'm not a good person?" "That I'm a bad mother?" "That I lied to him?"

In the example with Kate and Jane:

The conversation makes Jane question, "Am I a bad boss?"

Kate questions, "Am I a bad worker? Does my boss think I'm lazy?"

Going back to *your* difficult conversation, let's first do the basic analysis.

Diagnosis: What Made the Conversation Difficult?

1. The "What Happened?" Conversation

One thing that makes conversations difficult is when two people have different versions of the facts at issue. Looking back at your difficult conversation, what was your side of the story?

_____

_____

_____

Okay, now it's time for you to be imaginative. Does your conversation partner have a different version of "the facts"? You don't have to have majored in literary theory or physics to know that the facts often look different from different points of view—and what facts "really" matter differ too. Take it as a working assumption that the other person is not clueless or malevolent. People sometimes are, but most people aren't. They are being a pain because they literally see things differently. If your goal is to communicate with them, you need to stop defining your viewpoint as Truth and their viewpoint as Falsehood.

Note: if your conversation partner in the difficult conversation was really, truly just an evil person lying, choose another difficult conversation for the remainder of this exercise.

What "really" happened from the other person's point of view?

_____

_____

_____

_____

_____

_____

2. The Feelings Conversation

Step 2 is to figure out whether the conversation became difficult because one or both of you had feelings you were not acknowledging.

If it really was a difficult conversation, more than likely there were strong feelings on both sides. What were they on yours? Examples: "I felt like she was calling me a liar"; "He made me feel worthless"; "He takes my good work and never gives me any praise or encouragement."

_____

_____

_____

_____

_____

_____

Okay, you know the drill. Now it's time to use your imagination. What feelings do you think might have driven the behavior of your conversation partner?

_____

_____

_____

_____

_____

_____

3. The Identity Conversation

Step 3 is to figure out whether the conversation turned so difficult because it triggered, in one or both of the conversation partners, an "identity quake."[2] That's when you, in the course of the conversation or because of its nature—think performance evaluation—feel that a fundamental aspect of your identity is threatened.

Here's a classic example: Let's say you get negative feedback on a performance evaluation. If you interpret it as an attack or as a global assertion that you are lazy or stupid, the natural reaction is to resist taking in the feedback. This is perilous. You need to listen carefully to negative feedback, identify what skills you need to step up, and then get information about how to accomplish that. None of that will happen if you hear "global attack" and go into a defensive crouch.

Now go back to your original difficult conversation. Did it produce an identity quake for you?

_____

_____

_____

_____

_____

Did the difficult conversation produce an identity quake for your conversation partner?

_____

_____

_____

_____

_____

Action Plan: A Path Out

1. The "What Happened?" Conversation

As you can see, most of what makes conversations difficult is a failure of imagination: a failure to be able to imagine how the facts look from someone else's point of view, what they are feeling or how you have threatened a cherished identity they hold.

Return to the "what happened?" conversation. How do you find out whether your conversation partner sees things differently? You ask them. And then you say, "Wow, that's different from the way things look from my point of view. Here's how I have been thinking about this. Now I see that you see things very differently."

Again following the *Difficult Conversations* formula, this requires three shifts:[3]

A. MOVING FROM CERTAINTY TO CURIOSITY

Rather than being certain that your truth is *the* truth and that things won't end well unless the other person adopts your version of the truth, be curious to hear and understand their version of the truth.

B. DISENTANGLING INTENT FROM IMPACT

You need to be *really* careful about characterizing other people's intent. The fact is you cannot know other people's intent. What you can know is what impact their statements had on you. Then the door is open for them to articulate whether they intended that or whether they choose not to disclose their intent and address your concern in a different way.

C. MAP WHAT EACH OF YOU CONTRIBUTED TO GET THINGS TO WHERE THEY NOW STAND

Rarely or never is only one person to blame when a conversation goes off the rails. Typically, both people contributed. What was your contribution? Note: It's far better to dispense with the language of blame. That language was designed for a take-no-prisoners, zero-sum-game, I'm-right-or-you're-right mentality, which is what we are trying to get away from.

Let's go to another difficult conversation at work to do this exercise—one that hasn't happened yet. (We'll do one about a nonwork matter later.)

How will you move from certainty to curiosity—what exactly will you say? Remember, you have to *really* listen, not just pretend to be listening. It's not genuine, and is condescending, just to pretend. And it won't work.

Write here the ultradelicious "you're an idiot, this is what really happened" version. If Kate (from our example above) were to write this, she might say, "What really happened is that you are a terrible boss who can't keep track of when things are due, and you're trying to cover up the fact that you're disorganized by blaming it all on me." Now you try:

_____

_____

_____

_____

_____

_____

Now write the Sober Adult "this is what I saw, what did you see?" version. Kate might say, "From my point of view, I saw that there was a miscommunication about the deadline for the assignment and a lack of communication about what the priority was." Now you go:

_____

_____

_____

_____

_____

Remember, don't characterize other people's intent. To do this, focus on how the person's actions *impacted you*. Check your assumptions about the intent behind those actions at the door.

Write a "this is how what you said impacted me" version of the conversation. Jane might say, "When you turned in the assignment late, it impacted my ability to get it to the client on time, which reflects badly on not just me but our whole company."

_____

_____

_____

_____

_____

_____

Now let's learn how to map what you each contributed to the end result of having the conversation go off the rails. Write here the ultradelicious "it's all your fault." Kate might say, "Because you never communicated to me the exact deadline for the assignment, it is your fault that you turned it in to the client late."

_____

_____

_____

_____

_____

Now write a version that identifies what you contributed that helped the conversation go off the rails. Hopefully, Jane would say, "The instructions I gave you weren't clear, and I wasn't communicating with the other supervisors about how much was on your plate." And Kate might say, "I didn't double check with you to see if there was a specific deadline, and I didn't give you a heads-up that I had to prioritize other projects."

_____

_____

_____

_____

_____

TROUBLE SHOOTING: "SO GLAD WE AGREE YOU'RE AN IDIOT"
Key question: what if you're brave and honest and admit your contribution, only to have the other person say, "Hey, glad you agree with me that you acted like a jerk / were just so wrong it's pathetic / are a wimp for giving in / glad I won."

Does that mean this formula doesn't work?

Nope.

First, it's our belief that won't happen very often—if it does, you may need to find new friends or a new workplace. If you make yourself vulnerable by acknowledging your behavior wasn't perfect, most people will immediately or quickly stop fighting and admit they aren't perfect either. If they don't, you've found out something super important about them.

Second, make sure you've given the person adequate time to back off. Try these strategies:

✓ Give them more than one opportunity to move from a defensive crouch. "I have really tried to be honest with myself about what happened and have tried to see where I contributed to things going off the rails. I would really appreciate hearing about it if you think you contributed in any way."

✓ Keep asking questions to reassure the person you are paying attention to their version of what happened. Paraphrase what you hear and ask if you have it right. "I hear that you think I did X for Y reason. Have I got that right? No wonder you were upset with me."

✓ Signal that you have an open mind. "I'm surprised to hear you say that. It makes me feel a bit defensive, but I would love to understand better what you mean."[4]

✓ Acknowledge some validity in what they are saying if you can. "If I felt someone had lied to me, I would be angry, too. This is how things looked from my point of view."

✓ Mirror back what the person is saying. "What I'm hearing you say is [paraphrase what they said]. Did I get that right?"

✓ Ask for more concrete information.[5] "Can you give me some examples? I would like to understand better how things look from your point of view."

✓ Don't press the person for an answer; know when to take a break.[6]

If you've tried all that, and the person insists on a zero-sum, so-glad-you've-admitted-it's-your-fault game, shift to damage-control mode. Stop trying to resolve the conflict, and figure out who in your environment needs to know that you had an honest disagreement with this person. It's best to frame this as "Don't need to drag you into this, but X and I had a difference of opinion, and I want you to know the lay of the land." Don't name-call. Dispassionately describe the disagreement, describing the other person in a respectful way. That way, if that other person describes you as Darth Vader, it's going to be pretty obvious who is being coolheaded.

One of the most important pieces of advice Joan has ever received is this: remember, if someone is a bully, you're not the only person who knows it! (Many thanks to Michele Coleman Mayes.)

2. Avoiding Identity Quakes

Even business disagreements sometimes have a strong emotional load, and disagreements in private life often do. Ask yourself, are strong feelings making the conversation difficult?

If so, the first step is to ask yourself whether one or both of you is having an identity quake. Is your identity as a good person or a competent one being placed at risk? Is the other person's? If so, you've got to find a way to parse things out: this is a business disagreement about a business issue, not a global judgment about someone's intrinsic worth.

If you feel that things have gotten off the rails, here are some tools to help you address this directly.

IF THE OTHER PERSON IS HAVING AN IDENTITY QUAKE

✓ Clearly identify that the disagreement is over one specific issue and not the person's identity as a good person. "Although we disagree, I respect that you are trying to do what's best for the company. You are always so conscientious that when you have a hesitation, I really listen up." (Say something that's true and that you believe.)

✓ Clearly identify the specific issue and reaffirm the person's identity as competent. "I really benefit from your expertise and thoughtfulness—you bring so much to the table. Here's why I disagree with your assessment in this case."

IF IT'S YOU HAVING THE IDENTITY QUAKE

Try to separate out the feedback you're receiving from the part of your identity that it's affecting.

What is the fear that the disagreement is triggering (e.g., "That I'm a bad person" or "That I'm bad at my job")?

_____

_____

_____

_____

_____

_____

Now revisit the disagreement. What did the person actually say?

_____

_____

_____

_____

_____

_____

Can you see the difference between the two?

If you're upset, you can always ask for some time. Step away from the emotion of the disagreement and revisit it later.

Once you've addressed any identity quake issues, you need to find a way to defuse other strong emotions. Here are some ways to do so:

✓ Acknowledge their feelings. "It seems like this is really important to you." "It sounds like you are really angry about what's happened."
✓ Give them time to cool off. If they are red-hot angry, often it's best to take a break. "You've given me a lot to think about. I want to think through why we see this so differently. Then I'll get back to you, and we can continue to think this through together. Make sense?"
✓ Describe the impact of their actions on you. "I'm feeling really attacked right now, though I don't think that's your intention."

3. Avoiding Common Pitfalls

WHAT IF SOMEONE ACCUSES YOU OF LYING?

First of all, don't lie. Not only is it unethical, but it's virtually impossible to do convincingly: you have to keep track of what you've said to whom, and things get really complicated really quickly. The most common form of lying is when people misrepresent things to others because they aren't being honest with themselves. If you think that might be the case, then go to your network (see part 3, "Networks") and do a reality check. Being honest with yourself today, even if it's painful, is far less painful than having to deal with having people think they can't trust you.

If you're caught in a lie, there is really only one choice: *admit it*. "I am really sorry. That showed really bad judgment. I have learned from my mistake, and I will never do it again. Sorry you had to be the one to teach me that important lesson."

What if someone sincerely believes you have lied, but you are convinced you haven't—and have done a reality check with trusted advisers who agree with you? Explain why you and the person who disagrees with you see things differently.[7] "I can see why you are upset—I would be, too, if I thought someone had lied to me. But I should explain that I did *not* lie: we are holding different parts of the elephant. Here's how things look from my point of view."

WHAT IF SOMEONE GIVES YOU A NEGATIVE PERFORMANCE EVALUATION?

First, thank them for being so honest with you. One pattern that particularly affects people of color is that white people are not honest with them for fear of being seen as racist. Sometimes men aren't honest with women, either, for fear that the women will cry or that they will be called sexist. At the same time, as we discussed, stereotypes and the four patterns of bias can also impact how people of color and women are viewed. If you think you are being dinged because you are a woman and/or a person of color, think through whether you could make it work to call out the bias. (Read with "Strategy 4: Address the Bias—With Kid Gloves?" on pages 51–53 of *What Works*.) If you can't call it out, consider turning to part 7, "Leave or Stay?," and considering whether it's time for you to move on.

But let's say you just got a crummy performance review. We all get them from time to time. What's the second step? Shut up and listen. Do not try to justify yourself. If upon reflection you believe the evaluation is unfair, you can contest it later. In real time, present yourself as someone who is open and attentive to developmental feedback.

Third, make sure you understand what the person is saying. If you don't understand or agree with their assessment, ask for specific examples of the behavior at issue. If they can't think of any examples, shame on them—they should have these at their fingertips. But don't tell them that: instead, say, "It would be really helpful to me if, the next time that happens, you let me know immediately so I can address it right away."

Fourth, tell the person what steps you will take to address the developmental feedback and ask for permission to check in so you can be sure your steps have been effective. "Thanks so much for your honesty. Is it okay if the next time I hand a memo in, we have a quick check-in to make sure my performance is up to snuff?"

Fifth, if you think the feedback is unfair, listen attentively in real time and then go to your network for a reality check (see part 3, "Networks"). Contesting negative feedback as unfair is a big step. Before you take that step, decide first whether you just want to leave quietly or transfer to a different department (see part 7, "Leave or Stay?"). If you decide to take that step, consult carefully with the trusted advisers in your network about how to do so without having the situation blow up in your face.

WHAT IF YOU CRY?

Crying usually is not considered appropriate in the workplace because it demands that the other person deal with your strong emotions, which is not something we typically ask of each other at work. There's also sexism: crying is considered a sign of weakness. It ain't necessarily so, but whatever. If you feel like you're going to cry, usually the best thing to do is to thank the person for the feedback, say you need some time to think carefully about it, and ask if you can take a break and continue the meeting later. If you can manage to do this without breaking down, your self-control will be admired.

What if you break down or don't make it to the ladies' room in time? It's not the end of the world. Just say something like, "I'm really disappointed to hear that my performance has been lacking. I'm upset now; can we take a break and continue this conversation later?"

Have you ever had a negative performance evaluation? How did you handle it?

_____

_____

_____

_____

_____

_____

Based on the advice in this chapter, would you handle it differently today? If so, how so?

_____

_____

_____

_____

_____

_____

_____

_____

_____

_____

Okay, now it's time to apply the *Difficult Conversations* model to a nonwork conversation.

19

Negotiating Work-Family Conflict

(Including How to Choose a Partner Who's Really a Partner)

One common source of tension in professional women's lives is work-family conflict. This chapter talks you through that difficult conversation, including how to choose a partner who'll really be a partner—the single most important step to avoiding work-family conflict in the future. Much of our advice in this chapter deals with work-family conflict in heterosexual relationships, often with children, as these are family situations in which gender bias challenges commonly arise. However, the exercises in this chapter for helping to deal with work-family conflict at home are designed to help all families, and women in same-sex and child-free partnerships will benefit from these exercises as well.

Women often assume that the way to avoid getting stuck sacrificing a career they love in order to have the family they want is to marry a man who believes in equality for women.

Wrong answer.

The key is not to choose a partner who feels that, if you really love him, you will support his ability to be as successful as his taste and talents enable him to be. A man like that can believe in women's equality until the day he dies. But he doesn't believe in *your* right to have a career equal to his own. He thinks he is entitled—and perhaps required—to have you play a supporting role: to raise his kids while he focuses on his career.

That may be just fine with you. If it is, no judgment. Raising children is honorable work. But being home full-time is not the chief career goal of most professional women: one study found that only 16 percent of highly trained professional women who became stay-at-home mothers always intended to do so.[1]

A much-larger group gave up their careers because their husbands did not support them. "He always says, 'You can do anything you want,' but he's never there to pick up any of the load," said one.[2]

We can readily see that one reason conversations around work and family become so fraught is because they produce identity quakes: "Am I a good mother?" "Am I a man to be reckoned with?" "What does it mean to be a good father?"

A great book to help you navigate these waters is Sharon Meers and Joanna Strober's *Getting to 50/50*. We can't recommend it highly enough. Here are a few pointers.

How to Choose a Partner Who'll Really Be a Partner

The key is to find out whether your partner believes in equality for women, full stop, or whether he feels a need, and an entitlement, to be an ideal worker who is always available for work, in a career where he can go as far as it can take him. He may feel he needs to be free to perform as an ideal worker because he loves his work or because he will feel like a loser unless he has a super-successful career or because he feels *you* will see him as a loser if he doesn't—or the world will. All are common reasons men refuse to do the kinds of things children need that often interfere with work, from leaving work for a well-baby visit to leaving early to drive a child to soccer to taking family leave or cutting back on work hours.

It's helpful to talk through concrete situations. Here are some conversation starters:

1. "**What if the baby was sick, and you and I both had an important meeting? How would we figure out who would stay home?**"
2. "**What if money was tight, and I wanted to enroll in a leadership skills development training and you wanted to buy a car? How would we decide how to spend our money?**"

Handling Work-Family Conflicts

Step 1: Get Over Yourself

Are you a good mother or a selfish career woman? Is he a good husband or a hypocritical sexist? The reasons work-family conflicts escalate so much is that they go deep into some of our most cherished identities.

The first step is to realize that the culture sets us up for grief. The cultural ideal is of a worker who is always available for work and of a mother who is always available for her children.[3] Folks, this is impossible. The culture also intimates that a man who is not "all in" at work is a wimp.[4] Raise your hand if you want your husband to be less of a man.

In a quiet moment, ask yourself whether you as a professional woman are holding yourself up to the standard set by your own stay-at-home mother. If you are, that's not realistic. You are turning motherhood into a performance test, which is not the way to produce well-adjusted children. You have learned to know what they want and accept who they are. You must do this with yourself.

One businesswoman told us, "You just can't do all the little things your mother probably did. And you have to pick and choose and decide what's going to give you joy and passion—and that will be important to your children—and what just doesn't matter that much."[5]

Within broad limits, what you do matters less than the emotional tone of what you do does. If you do everything your mom did, feeling rushed and pressured and inadequate all the time, then that's what you are modeling for your children. If you do a lot less, but if you, serenely and mindfully, do what gives you pleasure, then that's the model of adulthood your kids will see. You choose.

Name some things that you love to do with your children:

_____

_____

_____

_____

_____

_____

Joan loved taking her kids to the park or zoo, so she did that once a week throughout the time they were little. She loved bath time; some people hate it. She love-hated getting up at 5:30 a.m. with her son, who woke up then like clockwork. Joan and her husband switched off, which got her more in touch with the love and less with the hate. Looking back, she probably should have cooked a full, homemade dinner less often.

Marina's mom loved having family dinners and reading to her kids at night. She enjoyed going to the school plays, ballet recitals, and soccer games (bless her heart). But she didn't love doing all the driving, so she split driving with Marina's dad and hired a nanny to fill in the cracks.

Name here some things you just don't enjoy doing with your kids:

_____

_____

_____

_____

_____

_____

Does your partner (or someone else in your household) enjoy what you don't? If so, there's your answer. If not, can you afford to hire help to do the things you don't enjoy? Marina's parents hired someone to do the grocery shopping, mail sending, and dry cleaning for a period of time when things were especially hectic. Could you do this?

_____

_____

_____

_____

_____

If you can't hire help, how can you simplify? Remember, if you're doing what you really hate just because you think you should, how will that help your child's self-esteem?

_____

_____

_____

_____

_____

_____

Step 2: Getting to 50/50
(With thanks to *Getting to 50/50* by Sharon Meers and Joanna Strober)

Conflicts over who will do the work of the family tend to sharply increase after the birth of children.[6] Research reports that sharing housework more evenly between partners is one of the top-two predictors of how happy a woman is in her marriage[7] and decreases the chance the couple will divorce by up to 50 percent.[8]

Why, then, does it seem so hard to reach an even distribution? Why are partners who truly love each other so unwilling to hear each other out and to change? See "Step 3: Defusing Identity Quakes."

Are you doing more than your fair share? Most women are. Men's household contributions have increased, but women still do twice as much routine housework as men do.[9] They also do twice as much child care—particularly the kind that interrupts work hours.[10]

Some women, faced with recalcitrance at home, carry 100 percent of the load and demand that their work colleagues pitch in to help cover for them. Unless you have formally decreased your hours, this is not fair to your colleagues at work. It means that you have twice as many family demands as you otherwise would and can quickly wear out your colleagues' patience.

The first step in getting to 50/50 is to come to an agreement with your partner about what needs to get done. A common mistake mothers make is to treat their version of what needs to get done as nonnegotiable.

Some things are, of course: leaving a young child alone in a bathtub for even a minute; leaving a toddler alone at the top of the stairs; leaving dishes in the sink until they get green and smelly. These basic issues are nonnegotiable.

But most things are not nonnegotiable. Here are examples:

1. Whether the bed is made neatly (or at all)
2. Driving kids to a different after-school enrichment activity every day
3. Having a home-cooked meal every night

4. Making cupcakes from scratch for a child's birthday (decorating store-bought ones will please kids just as much)

5. Enforcing a "no screens" rule every second of the day

6. Having a parent attend every single school function or sports game

7. Whether clothes are strewn on the floor or neatly folded

8. Having a clean house all the time

Mothers are under hydraulic societal pressures to display selfless dedication to children's needs regardless of their personal well-being—and to be Martha Stewart to boot. Men aren't under these pressures, and we need to learn from them. Because when we go into our baking-cupcakes-until-two-a.m. frenzies, what we are displaying for our children is that conscientious people live lives governed by anxious performance pressure. Are you really baking those cupcakes for your kids or for an imagined audience of the other mothers?

We're not talking about situations where you bake as a fun way to bond with your kids or because you find it relaxing. We're talking about situations where you are exhausting yourself Martha Stewart–ing your poor unsuspecting life.

Get over yourself.

Your partner is not under this kind of performance pressure. Frankly, sometimes his judgment on what's needed may be better than yours.

Insisting that your partner do things exactly the way you would is called *gatekeeping*. It's a sure way to discourage him from participating.

Here's a threshold issue before you begin: Do you have a date night? You need one every week or two. If you can't afford babysitting, swap babysitting with some friends so they can have date night, too. On date night, you need to have a date—not a negotiation. Remember when you took time out to enjoy each other's company and please each other? That's called dating. It's not over. Date night is fun, but it's also important. It keeps you in touch with why you're still together. It doesn't have to be expensive. A walk and a picnic works in the summer.

The best approach is to begin a series of conversations with your partner (I'll call him your husband) that communicates that getting to 50/50 is very important to you, in a tone that's "affectionate though unmovable," to quote *Getting to 50/50*.[11] Getting the tone right is crucial. Many of the most satisfied couples disagree on a regular basis. "The key issue is not *whether* a couple argues, but *how*."[12] That's where the *Difficult Conversations* model comes in. It requires you to engage in good faith, not to assume you're totally in the right and he's totally in the wrong, and to *listen*. Remember, this is your husband you're talking to, not "some no-show house painter, so treat him accordingly."[13]

Women historically have been trained to complain and comply. This is not the way to get your way, and it's not a great model for the kids to see, either. If that's been the tone of these conversations in the past, reassure your partner that that will end. You'll both feel better if you come to an agreement where you each ask for what you want explicitly and reach a compromise you both can live with for a period of time, with a mutual pact not to kvetch or criticize in the meantime.

This approach begins with a difficult conversation, *and with an open mind*, about what housework and child care needs to get done. The goal is to agree on an important initial question: 50/50 of what?

Here's how to start. Have both you and your partner write down, on one side of a piece of paper, all the housework you do. On the other side, write down everything your partner does. Then do the same thing for child care, putting an asterisk on items you do for the kids that mean that you have to take time off work.

Here are the forms:

The List

Here's the housework I do:

_____

_____

_____

_____

_____

_____

_____

_____

_____

_____

Here's the housework my partner does:

_____

_____

_____

_____

_____

_____

_____

_____

_____

_____

_____

Here's the child care I do:

_____

_____

_____

_____

_____

_____

_____

_____

_____

_____

_____

Here's the child care my partner does:

_____

_____

_____

_____

_____

_____

———————————————————————————

———————————————————————————

———————————————————————————

———————————————————————————

———————————————————————————

Once both you and your partner have filled out The List, compare your lists. You will notice that we are back at the *Difficult Conversations* "what happened?" conversation. Have your partner present his List, compare it to your List, and respectfully and without accusation talk about how to get to 50/50, using these principles:

1. What is one partner doing that they don't enjoy that the other partner would enjoy doing?

———————————————————————————

———————————————————————————

———————————————————————————

———————————————————————————

———————————————————————————

———————————————————————————

2. If there are things neither parent enjoys, are they really necessary? For example, if you are being driven nuts driving kids to a million activities, how about a rule that each child can choose one sport and one other activity at a time? If cooking dinner means a high-stress evening, can you get tamales once a week at the farmers' market, have hamburgers one night, and cook a stew over the weekend for the other nights? Keep in mind: what kids will remember is the emotional tone, not what was on the menu.

———————————————————————————

———————————————————————————

———————————————————————————

———————————————————————————

———————————————————————————

3. Once you have simplified your life, can you afford to hire someone to do those things that are left that neither parent enjoys? If not, is there a relative who might enjoy doing them? Or a close friend? What could you give the person helping you that might be of value to them, to maintain a sense of reciprocity?

_____

_____

_____

_____

_____

4. Okay, what's left are things neither parent enjoys but that really, truly need to get done. How can you switch off so that no one has to do them all the time? Recall Joan's solution of switching off getting up at 5:30 a.m. with her husband. Once she did not have to do it every single day, she began to look forward to her early-morning walk with her son.

_____

_____

_____

_____

_____

5. Now make a new List of what you will do and what your partner will do. These need to cover everything you have both agreed needs to get done, in a way that allocates the work fairly.

_____

_____

_____

_____

_____

_____

6. Set up a time to revisit The List—three or six months is about right. Now stop second-guessing yourself. You need the self-discipline to say, "Either I am going to do this because I want to, or I won't do it. I will not do it angry." That means you need to keep at your difficult conversation with your partner until you come to a true agreement.

7. Set up sanctions if one party does not do what they have promised. Examples: The other party gets to go out for a night on the town with friends. The other party gets to go to the gym every Saturday morning. Don't make it punitive; make it a reward for the one who remained true to The List. Keep blame out of it. Just, "Hey, I'm hoping you've neglected X on The List on purpose. I'm already planning to party."

_____

_____

_____

_____

_____

_____

8. Remember the formula, "When I see dirty socks on the floor, I feel . . ." and then give a sincere description in a measured tone; snake venom's less useful.[14]

What if you still get in constant disagreements over whether or not one party has kept to The List? Time for a marriage counselor. This type of conflict is a chief cause of divorce.

Step 3: Defusing Identity Quakes

There is no one way to be a perfect mother, but a million ways to be
a good one.
—Jill Churchill

Remember the Martha Stewart–cupcake moment discussed earlier? What was going on there?

Most women feel pretty passionately that they want to be good a mother—the June Cleaver in our heads. Sometimes, it's the desire to live up to the example set by our stay-at-home mothers or our mothers who went part-time when we were young. What are the old tapes about motherhood swirling around in you? Where do they come from?

_____

_____

_____

_____

_____

_____

Are those old tapes consistent with your career goals?

_____

_____

_____

_____

_____

If not, how could you nip and tuck, to construct a new model of motherhood that fits better with your career goals? Here are some facts to help you:

1. Within broad limits, what matters is not whether a mother works or stays home but whether she is happy with the work-life balance she's created.
2. Traditionally, children were raised by groups of adults—which is what you are creating when you create a caring circle that includes your nanny or child-care center, your kids' teachers and coaches, and so on. Different adults can offer different things to kids. (News flash: things you often cannot offer.)
3. Remember, your children will sense it if you are anxious, time starved, or overwhelmed. The easiest way to be not a good-enough mother is to insist on being a perfect one.

Okay, time for your new version of your own mothering ideal:

_____

_____

_____

_____

_____

_____

Now it's time for your partner. For this chapter, I'll assume it's a man. In gay couples, there may be more variation.

Most men feel pretty passionately that they want to be a good father—and a "successful man." What is a successful man? Traditionally, that's defined by career success. That means that many men feel under intense internal pressure to compete with the successful men around them—often men who are breadwinners married to homemakers.

That's often the reason why men are so reluctant to get to 50/50.

Is this how you define the "successful man"?

_____

_____

_____

_____

_____

_____

How about your husband?

_____

_____

_____

_____

_____

If that's not how you define success, does your husband know that? If not, how can you communicate it?

_____

_____

_____

_____

_____

Another reason men are reluctant to get to 50/50 is that they fear that they will be seen as less ambitious, or less manly, if they take time off for family reasons. Alas, this may not be an irrational fear. Studies on the "flexibility stigma" report that men who take family leave or request flexible work arrangements often are seen as less promotable—because they are seen as too feminine.[15] Does your husband have this fear?

_____

_____

_____

_____

_____

Discuss with your husband whether he feels unable to get to 50/50 and keep his present job. What are his thoughts about that?

_____

_____

_____

_____

_____

Would you prefer he leave his job if that's the case, even if that means sacrificing income?

_____

_____

_____

_____

_____

How could you start a conversation about this? Keep in mind that one path that many parents take is to keep doing the same type of work as before but as a consultant or in a new business model that allows for better work-family balance. For an inventory of this type of organization for lawyers, check out the report by Joan C. Williams, Aaron Platt, and Jessica Lee called "Disruptive Innovation: New Models of Legal Practice."[16]

Increasingly, many men feel that being a good father means being involved with the daily care of their children. (This is why men are reporting increased levels of work-family conflict.)[17] This is in sharp contrast to more traditional models that define the good father as someone who does a good job of supporting his family. How does your husband define being a good father?

_____

_____

_____

_____

_____

_____

If your husband is experiencing work-family conflict, then The List exercise should improve his standard of living as well as yours.

PART VI

Talking across Race about Gender Bias

For women of color, it's more complicated . . . or not. Kori Carew, Jean Lee, Jessica Lee, Isabelle Salgado, and Amber Williams all contributed to this part. Many thanks to them for their expertise.

In our interviews for *What Works for Women at Work,* women of color were more likely to report each of the four patterns of gender bias than white women were. Here are the numbers, arranged from the largest to the smallest differences:

1. Tug of War: 59 percent of women of color, 50 percent of white women
2. Tightrope: 77 percent of women of color, 68 percent of white women
3. Maternal Wall: 63 percent of mothers of color, 56 percent of white mothers
4. Prove-It-Again!: 70 percent of women of color, 64 percent of white women

One big difference between white women and women of color is that white women don't have the added pressure of being a racial minority. This part will help you think through how to deal with a few common kinds of racism in ways that help prevent it from hurting your career. Even if you don't fill out the sections that are about another race, we encourage you to take the time to read through them.

In addition, a survey of women of color scientists found that different groups reported very different experiences with gender bias. Here are the key differences:

1. Black women were far more likely to report Tug of War and Prove-It-Again!: 75 percent of all women reported, "Women in my environment generally support each other," but only 56 percent of black women agreed.[1] Black women also were far more likely to report Prove-It-Again!: 77 percent of black women reported it, but only about 66 percent of women in general did.[2]
2. Asian American women were far more likely to report pressure to behave in feminine ways and more pushback if they didn't: 41 percent of Asian American women reported pressure to behave in feminine ways; 61 percent reported pushback for being assertive.[3] (For comparison, only 8 percent of black women reported pressure to behave in feminine ways; 54 percent reported backlash for being assertive.)[4]
3. Latina women reported the most pushback for showing anger and the largest loads of office housework: 60 percent reported backlash for showing anger (as compared to roughly 50 percent of women in general).[5] Latina women, in interviews, appeared to have large loads of office housework.

This part discusses how gender bias differs by race.

20

Black Women

📖 (Read with pages 226–238 of *What Works*)

Social Isolation

Black women scientists were far more likely than other women to report a sense of social isolation.[1] This included reports about feeling excluded from office social activities and feeling alienated from colleagues.[2] Is that something you've experienced?

_____

_____

_____

_____

_____

If social isolation has not affected you, skip to the next section.

One obvious reason for this sense of isolation is that many black professionals are in environments where they are the only black professional in sight—they are literally more isolated.[3] Is that true of you?

_____

_____

_____

_____

_____

If you don't have a network of people you click with at work, what are some other ways you can fulfill that need for companionship of people like you? Some ideas are church, clubs, or a professional organization aimed at your group. List here at least three ways you could find the companionship you need in your own community.

_____

_____

_____

_____

_____

A happy circumstance of the modern world is that we can also gain sustenance from networks that are not based on geographical proximity. For example, you could join a national professional organization. Here are some examples:

American Association of Blacks in Energy
Association of Black Psychologists
Black Culinary Alliance (BCA)
Black Data Processing Associates
Blacks in Government
Executive Leadership Council
Joint Center for Political and Economic Studies
National Association of African Americans in Human Resources
National Association of Black Accountants
National Association of Black Journalists
National Association of Blacks in Criminal Justice
National Bar Association
National Black Business Council
National Black Business Trade Association
National Black Chamber of Commerce
National Black MBA Association
National Black Nurses Association
National Medical Association
National Organization for the Professional Advancement of Black Chemists and Chemical Engineers
National Organization of Black Law Enforcement Executives
National Sales Network
National Society of Black Engineers
National Society of Black Physicists
Organization of Black Designers
Student National Medical Association

Some of these organizations have mentoring programs that will link you with a mentor—often a wonderful opportunity. List at least three ways you could become part of a community outside your geographical area:

_____

_____

_____

_____

_____

Interviews suggest that another reason black professionals are more likely to report a sense of social isolation is that some may be more reluctant to drop their guard around people at work. One scientist explained why she did not socialize with her colleagues: "when you get to know people more socially, that's where the—to me, that lessens your authority."[4] Roughly 40 percent of black women reported, "I feel that socially engaging with my colleagues may negatively affect perceptions of my competence."[5] Do you share that fear?

_____

_____

_____

_____

_____

_____

Now run it through your head. Why do you hold this fear? Have there been instances in your professional career when this has happened?

_____

_____

_____

_____

_____

_____

Is there someone you trust whom you could talk this over with? Try to think of one to two people you trust who would be willing to lend an ear:

_____

_____

_____

_____

_____

_____

What one black biologist said indicates another possible dimension to the problem of social isolation: "So a lot of times, there are things that people exclude me from because they say, 'oh, she would be uncomfortable. . . .' They think for me . . . 'Oh, well, she's going to be the only Black person there. . . . Just don't invite her, she won't feel comfortable.'"[6] Do you think this might be going on in your environment? If so, and you would like to be included, brainstorm three low-key ways you can communicate that you would like to be included. These can include setting up social events as well as communicating your interest in those that already exist:

_____

_____

_____

_____

_____

_____

Racially Offensive Comments

"I didn't think much about it," said a biologist. "But I just thought it was strange that she just came out and told me that her parents just didn't like Africans Americans and that they still don't now and that when African Americans moved in their neighborhood during that time period that it was a lot of tension. And I was just like, oh, okay."[7]

Have you encountered racially offensive or racist comments at work? If so, give examples:

_____

_____

_____

_____

_____

_____

Growing up, how were you taught to deal with racially offensive comments or behaviors?

_____

_____

_____

_____

_____

Is that working for you in professional contexts?

_____

_____

_____

_____

_____

If it is not, try these:

✓ Say simply that your experiences are inconsistent with the stereotypes the speaker is referencing and that the better practice would be for the speaker not to speak of black people in that manner. Responding that "all people from X race are not like that" could come across as argumentative and inviting a debate about the validity of the stereotypes.

✓ Seek out mentors or colleagues who appear to be successfully navigating the environment, and get practical feedback and actionable advice about how you might respond differently.

✓ Script out and practice discussions with a trusted friend and colleague so you become more comfortable responding to racist comments less reactively.

✓ Think about tactics you might use to disengage or remove yourself from situations when someone is making racist comments, for example, saying, "Thank you for sharing your perspective," and then walking away.

✓ Is there someone else at work whom you trust, who could respond for you? Sometimes it's helpful to have an ally step in so you don't have to shoulder responding to all the offensive comments alone.

Black professionals, like other people of color, are often mistaken for administrative staff, lower-ranked professionals (e.g., paralegals or court reporters rather than lawyers), or custodians. (This even happens to scientists in lab coats!) Has that ever happened to you?

_____

_____

_____

_____

_____

_____

How did you handle that?

_____

_____

_____

_____

_____

_____

Did that strategy seem to work? If so, great. If not, can you think of a different one that might work better?

_____

_____

_____

_____

Here are some tips:

- ✓ Respond and clarify your status in a calm, nonconfrontational way, with a smile.
- ✓ Respond with a question: "That's fascinating. Why did you think I was a paralegal / lab tech / assistant?"
- ✓ Respond with humor: "I wouldn't choose pantyhose or this ugly rolling briefcase if I wasn't an attorney!"
- ✓ Find a trusted colleague or friend with whom you can share such experiences to help you work through frustrations and block internalization of the adverse emotional and psychological impact of such statements.

Again, should you have to be dealing with all this? Of course not. But until we can fix racism, let's keep developing strategies to navigate around it. (Note to Future Self: Fix racism.)

Prove-It-Again!

Black women scientists were far more likely than other women scientists to report Prove-It-Again! problems: 77 percent of black women did, as compared with 66 percent of women in general.[8]

Do you feel, in your workplace, that you have to prove yourself even more than white women do?

_____

_____

_____

_____

_____

Do you think the white women appreciate how different their experience is from yours?

_____

_____

_____

_____

_____

_____

Because black women may face more Prove-It-Again! bias than white women do in the workplace, you may need to use more of the strategies to combat this bias that we outlined in chapter 1 and in part 4, "Navigating Workplace Politics." Try not to internalize this bias—it's not a measure of your competence; it's a measure of the racial bias in your workplace. If you find all that you do is prove yourself over and over again, it may be time to look for another workplace (see part 7, "Leave or Stay?").

Tightrope

Black women scientists were far less likely to report pressure to behave in feminine ways than was any other group of women: only 8 percent did so.

Do you feel pressure to behave—or *not* behave—in feminine ways at your workplace?

_____

_____

_____

_____

_____

_____

If so, do you feel comfortable acceding to that pressure? Why or why not?

_____

_____

_____

_____

_____

_____

One wrinkle is that sometimes different people—or groups of people—have quite different perceptions of what is "feminine behavior." Have you encountered that?

_____

_____

_____

_____

_____

_____

If you don't want to go there, so be it. It's unfair that women should be pressured into feminine behavior.

If you feel comfortable using gender judo—doing something that's seen as masculine (like being assertive) in a feminine way—think about what from the toolkit of femininity you feel comfortable with: warmth, for example, or a focus on establishing an emotional connection. What are the aspects of femininity, if any, that you feel comfortable with that might be helpful in warding off the backlash commonly experienced by professional women who behave assertively or otherwise engage in behavior traditionally seen as masculine? See the "Gender Judo" section in the introduction for more.

_____

_____

_____

_____

_____

_____

Because black women face less pressure to behave in traditionally feminine ways, they may be able to get away with behaving in more traditionally masculine ways—except for showing anger. This is because one of the most powerful stereotypes of black people is of the "angry black woman."[9] Showing anger is risky for all women; it is probably riskier for black women. Do you feel comfortable expressing anger in your workplace?

_____

_____

_____

_____

_____

_____

Have you ever been accused of being "angry," when you felt you were merely asserting yourself?

_____

_____

_____

_____

_____

When you have shown anger at work, have you ever faced backlash?

_____

_____

_____

_____

_____

It is, of course, infuriating to be faulted for showing anger when that's used as a way of deflecting attention from the reason you were angered in the first place. If you've had that experience, how did you process it?

_____

_____

_____

_____

_____

This is an example of where your network is so important. Consult part 3, "Networks," if you don't have someone you can blow off steam with.

Maternal Wall

At WorkLife Law, where both Joan and Marina work, we hear persistent reports that women of color are denied flex schedules and other accommodations that are granted routinely to white mothers. (Note that this is illegal race discrimination.) Have you noticed this pattern or experienced it? If so, proceed with care—probably the best approach is to bring it up with human resources.

_____

_____

_____

_____

_____

Female lawyers of color are disproportionately the sole breadwinners in their families.[10] Are you the breadwinner in your household?

_____

_____

_____

_____

_____

_____

Have you ever encountered assumptions that you're not a breadwinner, if you are? Or that you are, if you're not?

_____

_____

_____

_____

_____

_____

Black mothers may have different notions about the role of their community in supporting child rearing than white mothers do. Has this ever caused tension or misunderstandings in your workplace?

_____

_____

_____

_____

_____

_____

Tug of War

In one survey, 75 percent of women in general reported that women in their workplaces generally supported each other—but only 56 percent of black women agreed.[11]

Do you feel that women in your workplace generally support each other?

_____

_____

_____

_____

_____

Some black women professionals report that white women pressure them into adopting traditionally feminine behaviors. Has this ever happened to you?

_____

_____

_____

_____

_____

This pressure from white women may stem from the fact that white women are themselves under pressure to behave in feminine ways—sometimes more pressure to do so than black women are.[12] If you have had this experience, how did you handle it?

_____

_____

_____

_____

_____

_____

Did that seem an effective way to handle the situation?

_____

_____

_____

_____

_____

As we mentioned before, black women and white women may have different ideas about what is "feminine behavior." How can you be authentic to yourself and your culture in a dominant majority organizational culture?

_____

_____

_____

_____

_____

21

Asian American Women

(Read with pages 246–252 of *What Works*)

Prove-It-Again!

One would think that the model minority stereotype, which depicts Asian Americans as hardworking and high achieving, would mean that Asian American women would be less likely than white women to face Prove-It-Again! problems. One study of scientists found that they were not: Asian American women science professors were as likely to report encountering it as white women were.[1]

Have you had that experience?

_____

_____

_____

_____

_____

_____

In addition to the strategies outlined in part 4, "Navigating Workplace Politics," here's another. One Asian American scientist we interviewed noted, "I'm more acceptable, if you will, as an Asian woman scientist rather than a woman scientist."[2] Have you seen this attitude in colleagues—or in yourself?

_____

_____

_____

_____

_____

_____

Particularly if you are in a field where Asian people "naturally excel"—science, technology, engineering, or math—consider finding subtle ways to remind people that you are Asian. This is annoying, for sure: reinforcing a stereotype. But our philosophy is that if these stereotypes are going to work against you—which they well may—you might as well deploy them strategically to work for you, too! Could you use this strategy in your workplace?

_____

_____

_____

_____

_____

_____

If you're in an environment where Asian American people are the majority (such as the Bay Area tech workforce),[3] this strategy may not work so well. We've heard that sometimes in fields where Asian American people are the majority group, there are expectations that you be "better than great" compared to your white counterparts.[4] If this situation applies to you, do you feel that pressure?

_____

_____

_____

_____

_____

_____

Walking the Tightrope

Asian American women were far more likely than women in general to report pressure to behave in feminine ways and more pushback if they didn't: 41 percent of Asian American women reported pressure to behave in feminine ways; 61 percent reported pushback for being assertive.[5] (For comparison, only 8 percent of black women reported feeling that pressure; 54 percent reported backlash for being assertive.)[6] Do you feel you have encountered pressure to behave in feminine ways? If so, how have you responded?

_____

_____

_____

_____

_____

_____

In addition to the stereotype that Asian American women are more feminine than white women are, Asian American women often are stereotyped as "passive," so people may try to take advantage of you on the theory that you won't put your foot down.[7] Has this happened to you?

_____

_____

_____

_____

_____

Asian American women also are more likely than other women to report pushback if they behave in traditionally masculine ways—that behavior may seem more transgressive in an Asian American woman if she is expected to be hyperfeminine.[8] Have you encountered comments that communicate that you "come on too strong," "should step back and give others a chance to shine," or are a "dragon lady" or that otherwise communicate disapproval that you are not living up to the stereotype that women should be modest, self-effacing, nice, and attuned to others' feelings?

_____

_____

_____

_____

_____

If you have encountered either pressure to behave in feminine ways or pushback if you don't, consider gender judo. See the "Gender Judo" section in the introduction for more.

Sometimes this can translate into expectations that Asian American people be "worker bees" who work hard, don't make demands, and aren't a good fit for leadership positions.[9] It can result in you being expected to work long hours—but not to get career-enhancing assignments or opportunities for leadership. (Note to Future Self: When in charge, make sure leadership reflects the company. No more diverse workforce with all white dudes running it.) Do you feel you've met this stereotype?

_____

_____

_____

_____

_____

_____

Some Asian American women have found that they can play into this stereotype to advance their careers. Again: annoying. Would you even consider that?

_____

_____

_____

_____

_____

_____

_____

Many Asian Americans have been brought up with the ethic that a good worker works hard and lets her work speak for itself. Is that true of you?

_____

_____

_____

_____

_____

_____

Sadly, if there are others out there working the politics, keeping your head down and just doing good work may not be enough. It's what our friend Carol Frohlinger calls "the tiara syndrome"—expecting that if you work hard, someone will walk up and put a tiara on your head.[10] Workplaces are political, which means that you need to be strategic if you want to get ahead. Otherwise, people will assume that you don't care whether you get ahead.

Effective strategies for escaping the worker-bee trap depend on the context. If you face expectations that you will work harder than those around you without making demands for advancement/leadership, keep in mind that this situation is working for everyone around you except you. If you don't put your foot down, those around you probably won't do it for you. After all, then they will have to work harder or will face more competition for coveted career-enhancing assignments or leadership positions. Does it feel hard to do this? If so, take the time to articulate why:

_____

_____

_____

_____

_____

Regardless of why it feels hard, you're going to have to step up and do it. Note that this may entail changing the expectations of the people around you. Here's a step-by-step guide:

1. You need to send the message that things need to change in a firm, measured, non-accusatory way. Who can help get you the kinds of opportunities you want? One approach is to ask that person or persons for a meeting about your two-year career goals. This can lead very naturally into a conversation about the kinds of work experiences you need to accrue, which can then lead to a conversation about how to transition you out of some of the kinds of things you are doing now. Work through how you would apply this strategy below—or suggest a different strategy:

_____

_____

_____

_____

_____

2. Don't wait until you're furious. Remember that showing anger often doesn't work well for women.[11] If you're already there, what's your strategy for cabining off your anger so it doesn't jeopardize your effectiveness?

_____

_____

_____

_____

_____

_____

3. Take ownership of the fact that you allowed this to continue, so the fault's not entirely with the people around you. Then think back: Were there any warning signs that you were approaching a breaking point? Can you identify any that led up to this point so you can try and deal with it earlier if it happens again?

_____

_____

_____

_____

_____

_____

Keep in mind that if there's no way you can get out of dead-end work, you need to think about looking for a new job. Refer to part 7, "Leave or Stay?"

Remember, it's always better to present a solution than a problem. Would some of the work you have been doing be a stretch assignment for someone more junior to you? If so, suggest them—but only do this if this work will genuinely be welcome. Otherwise, don't get yourself in the situation of suggesting someone for work no one wants. Write down the name of the person you could suggest, if there is someone, and why this work would be welcomed by them:

_____

_____

_____

_____

_____

_____

Another Tightrope issue is self-promotion. Many Asian American people were brought up with the "modesty mandate"—that good people are modest about their accomplishments.[12] Were you brought up with the sense that self-promotion is distasteful or worse?

_____

_____

_____

_____

_____

If so, hear this: in many workplaces, the squeaky wheel gets the oil. Others will be out there self-promoting. So if you don't, that will be interpreted in one of two ways. Either you aren't ambitious, or you are but don't care enough to put yourself out there. If neither of those is true, you need to let people around you know that you bring value. If you feel constitutionally uncomfortable with self-promotion, a good way to think about this is that you are saving people time: after all, it's narcissistic to assume that people should take time out of their already-busy days to ferret out evidence of your skills, goals, and accomplishments. That's not reasonable. It's your job to make it easy for them to advocate for you. So keep track of the objective metrics you've met and the compliments you're received. See chapters 1, 12, and 14 in the workbook for details.

It may be harder to do this as an Asian American woman because you may be judged by the default assumption that Asian Americans don't self-promote. Have you ever faced backlash—or heard of another Asian American employee at your workplace facing backlash—for self-promotion?

_____

_____

_____

_____

_____

Some people report to us that Asian American managers can be disapproving of other Asian American people if they engage in self-promotion, especially if they got to the position they're in without using self-promotion. Have you experienced this?

_____

_____

_____

_____

_____

We hear this is a tricky line to walk. It may not be worth it for you to engage in self-promotion if you've witnessed a strong culture of backlash against other Asian American employees at your workplace who self-promote. Or it may be that you're sick of waiting for a promotion and are willing to try. If you do, highlighting the objective metrics that you've met (see chapters 1 and 12 in the workbook) might be a safer place to start (focus on your quantitative—rather than qualitative—successes).

Maternal Wall

Asian American women scientists were more likely to report that their colleagues had communicated they should work fewer hours after having children (26.7 percent) than Latina scientists (9.1 percent) or black scientists (7.7 percent) were.[13] If you have children, have you felt that some of your colleagues assume that you should devote less time to your career now that you have kids?

_____

_____

_____

_____

_____

How do you deal with those types of assumptions?

_____

_____

_____

_____

_____

_____

Asian American scientists whom Joan interviewed related a couple of different ways that they handle workplace pressure to back off on their careers:

✓ Get together with other moms in your workplace[14]
✓ Reach out to your family for support (assuming they are in support of you pursuing your career while raising kids)[15]

If those strategies don't work or they're not feasible for your situation, it may be time to consider moving to a workplace that is more supportive of working parents. We know they exist. If you've hit the Maternal Wall at your workplace, it may be time to go. Read chapter 25 in the workbook if you think this may be your situation.

22

Latina Women

📖 (Read with pages 238–246 of *What Works*)

Prove-It-Again!

The vision of the scientist that is the White guy with the glasses and
that vision that if you ask a kid to draw me a scientist, they would
definitely draw a guy with glasses and White.
—Hispanic female, biomedical research[1]

All women often find they have to provide more evidence of competence than men do in order to be seen as equally competent, but the Prove-It-Again! problems reported by Latina science professors often included blatant insults, such as one woman's professor who, she recounted, "went as far as knocking on my head and saying, 'Is there anybody there?'" when she was a graduate student. Years later, her hands were shaking as she told the interviewer the story. "I was about 22 years old, so I went back to my office in tears." It took her years, she said, "just to be able to see myself again as somebody who actually did know what I was doing back then."[2]

A Latina scientist in geography thought that some people have "these kneejerk reactions that people of color or women of color aren't as competent."[3] A Latina scientist in biochemistry recounted being excluded when her (male) colleagues discussed her own project. When she suggested that it would have been appropriate to include her, they looked at her with surprise: "from that day on, I had to really fight and be very proactive about these things."[4]

Sometimes negative competence assumptions play out as hyperscrutiny. Said a biochemist, "They'll nitpick at the protocol, if that makes sense. Well, did you do something different? Did you change something on the protocol? Did you do it at a different time of day? Was the temperature exactly the same? You just have to address every one of their nitpicking questions, until you've answered them all. It's like, 'Okay, you're out of arguments.' Then they have to accept the fact that okay yes, you were successful in that, not because you're a woman, but because you can do the experiment, or you can do that project well."[5]

Have you had any similar experiences?

_____

_____

_____

_____

_____

_____

If so, how have you managed to avoid having this kind of experience shake your self-confidence?

_____

_____

_____

_____

_____

Some Latina women draw on the strength of their cultural traditions.[6] A biology professor noted, "I was raised in a culture where women are sort of stronger in a lot of ways. Women have learned to take over responsibility for their families and be the ones in charge. Whether you have a man or not, you have to make things happen. . . . I feel that that has given me strength in science where I don't believe paying much attention about what other people might think or not think and just go for what I think I want to do and that I need to do. I just don't give up. I'm from Puerto Rico."[7] A woman of Mexican descent agreed. "My mother is an extremely—she's a go-getter. My great-grandma grew up during the Mexican Revolution, and she was one of those ones that picked up guns and went fighting for the cause. It comes from generations of very assertive women."[8]

Are there people in your family whom you draw strength from?

_____

_____

_____

_____

_____

_____

How can you use those strengths at work to combat Prove-It-Again! bias?

_____

_____

_____

_____

_____

_____

Racial Stereotypes

Latina scientists also report meeting up with racial stereotypes. Most commonly, Latina women have encountered racial stereotypes about how "'you love tacos and you love spicy food'; 'Oh, you're very into drinking and music.'" And there are "jokes": "Oh, be careful. She's Puerto Rican and she may be carrying a knife in her purse."[9] A woman of Mexican heritage commented, "There seems to be a stereotype that, if you are from Mexico, you are lazy, and you only like to either sleep by a cactus or party. And I've really battled extremely hard all of these stereotypes."[10]

Have you encountered any racial stereotypes?

_____

_____

_____

_____

_____

_____

How did you respond? Was that response effective?

_____

_____

_____

_____

_____

_____

_____

If it wasn't, here are some suggestions:

✓ Say simply that your experiences are inconsistent with the stereotypes the speaker is referencing and that the better practice would be for the speaker not to speak of Latinos in that manner. Responding that "all people from X race are not like that" could come across as argumentative and invite a debate about the validity of the stereotypes.

✓ Seek out mentors or colleagues who appear to be successfully navigating the environment and get practical feedback and actionable advice about how you might respond differently.

✓ Script out and practice discussions with a trusted friend and colleague so you become more comfortable responding to racist comments less reactively.

✓ Think about tactics you might use to disengage or remove yourself from situations when someone is making racist comments, for example, saying, "Thank you for sharing your perspective," and then walking away.

✓ Is there someone else at work whom you trust, who could respond for you? Sometimes it's helpful to have an ally step in so you don't have to shoulder responding to all the offensive comments alone.

Latina scientists in lab coats also reported being mistaken for janitors or admins.[11] Has that ever happened to you? If so, what did you do? One scientist calmly informed her interrogator that she only had the key to her office, not to the janitor's closet.[12] Would something like that work for you?

_____

_____

_____

_____

_____

Here are some other tips:

✓ Respond and clarify your status in a calm, nonconfrontational way, with a smile.

✓ Respond with a question: "That's fascinating. Why did you think I was an admin?"

✓ Respond with humor: "I wouldn't choose pantyhose or this ugly rolling briefcase if I wasn't an attorney!"

✓ Find a trusted colleague or friend with whom you can share such experiences to help you work through frustrations and block internalization of the adverse emotional and psychological impact of such statements.

Tightrope

Interviews found that Latina women who behaved assertively risked criticism for being angry or "too emotional," even when the women themselves reported that they weren't angry—they just weren't deferential.[13] Nearly 60 percent of Latina women surveyed noted backlash for expressing anger, as compared with 54.4 percent of Asian American women, 49.7 percent of white women, and 47.8 percent of black women.[14]

In interviews, Latina women reported often being seen as angry when they were not. "I wasn't angry," noted one. "I just wasn't deferential."[15]

Have you encountered this stereotype?

_____

_____

_____

_____

_____

The line between asserting yourself and being angry is not always one people agree on. Have you experienced instances when there was a misunderstanding about this line or when you were told you were "angry" when you weren't?

_____

_____

_____

_____

_____

If so, how did you respond?

_____

_____

_____

_____

_____

_____

Did that strategy work well? If not, one approach is just to say, in the most neutral of tones, "I am not angry. We're just having a disagreement about business strategy." Would that work? Can you think of other statements you could try?

_____

_____

_____

_____

_____

In addition, in interviews, Latina scientists were far more likely than the other groups of women to report being expected—both by colleagues and by students—to do large loads of office housework, including literal housework (making coffee), administrative work typically performed by support personnel, and emotion work in helping students with their emotional problems.[16]

A Latina bioengineer reported being expected by her male faculty colleagues to "serve them tea or coffee or take notes."[17] A Latina woman in clinical science reported being expected to schedule meetings and do grant paperwork for her faculty colleagues—in effect, to act as their admin.[18]

Have you had similar experiences? If so, how have you handled them?

_____

_____

_____

_____

_____

If you want more ideas, refer to page 113 of _What Works_ for sassy comebacks in response to being asked to make coffee.[19]

Many of the Latina scientists interviewed spoke about dress. Most were acutely conscious that Latina women in general tend to dress more femininely and in more vivid colors than is the norm among white professional women. Some Latina women responded by "dressing vanilla" to counter the stereotype. Others celebrated their difference and felt that they had turned it to their advantage. "I happen to be a very girly girl," said another engineer. "I like high heels, I like cute dresses. Actually, that makes me stand out at conferences." She felt it worked to her advantage.[20]

Is the way you dress influenced by the fact that you're Latina? If so, how?

_____

_____

_____

_____

_____

_____

Whatever choice you make, make sure you do what makes you feel comfortable. "I will dress in the way that I feel comfortable, because if I'm dressed in a way that I'm not comfortable, my whole game is off," remarked an environmental engineer.[21]

Maternal Wall

Fully 69 percent of Latina women reported pressures from their families to have children, as compared with 60 percent of white women and 57 percent of black women.[22]

Latina women of Mexican descent were particularly vocal. Said a Latina biochemist, "Every good Mexican woman has kids in their 20s. Like I told you, I'm not following the norm with my culture. I address that like anything else. It's like it's my life, I will have kids when and if I want them."[23]

Have you encountered family pressures to have children? If so, how have you responded?

_____

_____

_____

_____

_____

_____

Some of the scientists also felt the pressure of traditions that place family work firmly in the province of the mother. "In terms of being a Hispanic mother . . . our culture expects women to definitely be the primary caregiver. . . . 99 percent of the work was my responsibility," said an immunologist.[24] A Latina doctor noted, "I feel like I have a very specific role in keeping my family running," a pressure she saw as self-imposed.[25]

Do you feel that you—or others—see the housework and child care as your sole responsibility?

_____

_____

_____

_____

_____

If so, we would urge you to reconsider. After all, it takes two to have a child—and evidence shows that children tend to do better when both parents play an active role.[26] As for the housework, consult chapters 19 and 27 in the workbook on work-family balance.

In addition to the family pressures, many Latina women reported Maternal Wall bias in their workplace. Said one Latina environmental engineer, "If you want to have a family, people do question how much you want your career."[27] Have you faced these sorts of questions in your workplace?

_____

_____

_____

_____

_____

See chapter 17 in the Workbook for strategies to deal with Maternal Wall bias. Pull out a few that you could apply in your workplace:

_____

_____

_____

_____

_____

Tug of War

Although only 18 percent of women scientists reported having trouble getting admins to do their work, this problem was far more common (36 percent) among Latina scientists.[28] Interviews suggested a racial dynamic: said one, "conscious or unconscious," there is resistance based on the fact that "there is this Mexican woman telling them what to do."[29]

Have you experienced this? How did you respond?

_____

_____

_____

_____

_____

_____

Probably the best approach is simply but firmly to insist on an equal level of support. If that doesn't work, you have a performance problem. Consult human resources about how to resolve the situation. The path of least resistance, if it's available, may be to switch admins.

23

White Women

As white women in the workplace (as both Joan and Marina are), we typically face gender but not racial bias. That is not to say we are not affected by racism—everyone is affected by racism; it's just not directed at us. How did you feel reading the preceding chapters? Were you aware that women of color face these issues?

_____

_____

_____

_____

_____

_____

We think that it is important for white women to know how gender bias differs by race for two reasons: (1) to be able to help when we can and (2) because gender bias affects white women differently than it does women of other races.

Interrupting Bias

As white women, we may be in the position to interrupt some of the racial bias that affects our female colleagues of color.

In the previous chapters, we outlined several of the specific issues facing women of color in the workplace. Have you noticed any of those issues where you work?

_____

_____

_____

_____

_____

_____

Have you noticed that gender bias affects you differently than it does your female colleagues of color?

_____

_____

_____

_____

_____

_____

Have you witnessed racism in your workplace or racially offensive comments or behaviors?

_____

_____

_____

_____

_____

How have you handled it?

_____

_____

_____

_____

_____

We don't pretend to have any solutions for racism, but we do think there may be some low-key ways that white women can interrupt it. After all, when racism is present in a workplace, it affects everyone, not just the people of color.

We described how 40 percent of the black female scientists we interviewed reported a sense of social isolation. Have you noticed that black women in your office are not as involved in social functions in your office?

_____

_____

_____

_____

_____

_____

This may be because the person doesn't want to participate or maybe doesn't get invited. You don't want to pressure someone to be involved if they don't want to be, but perhaps making sure you have extended the invitation would ease their sense of social isolation. Is this something you could do?

_____

_____

_____

_____

_____

Doing so could also be helpful for you in terms of expanding your network. Research shows that the most important factor in determining who you have in your network is similarity. Think about your network—is it mostly people who look like you?

_____

_____

_____

_____

_____

We're not implying that this has been a conscious choice of yours; it's a subconscious human tendency. Reaching out to black women in your office could increase the diversity in your network—which means access to different opportunities than you may otherwise have. (See part 3, "Networks," for more on this.)

We also discussed strategies for women of color to employ when they hear racist or racially offensive comments at the office. Do you ever hear these types of comments directed at or about your female colleagues of color?

_____

_____

_____

_____

_____

_____

If you do, it may be helpful for you to step in as an ally. We see a few options:

1. Respond to the person in the moment. Don't tell the person, "You're being racist," as that will trigger their defense mechanisms, and it could cause backlash for you. Instead, try to calmly but decisively convey that the person should stop talking: "Thanks for your perspective. Now, what were we talking about before?"

2. Pull the person who was making the racist comments aside after and explain your concerns to them. Again, tread carefully so as to not trigger the person's defensive mode. Try, "Earlier when you said X, it made me a little uncomfortable, and I'm afraid some people might take your comments as racially insensitive. I'm not calling you out, just giving you a heads-up for the future." Does that sound feasible?

3. If those steps would be too politically costly for you, an alternative (or additional) step could be approaching the woman of color in your office who heard the racist comments and offering your support. This won't stop the person from continuing with their comments, but it could help your colleague deal with them easier.

Prove-It-Again!

White women were less likely to report Prove-It-Again! bias (63 percent) than were women from other racial groups: black women (77 percent); Latinas (65 percent); Asian Americans (64 percent).[1] Have you noticed that Prove-It-Again! bias is more pervasive in your workplace against some groups than others?

_____

_____

_____

_____

_____

_____

Survey evidence shows that people of color, not just women, are more likely to experience the Stolen Idea than are white men.[2] We advise male allies to speak up when they see the Stolen Idea happening to women at work by saying something like, "I've been thinking about that ever since Michelle first said it. Tom, you've added something important. Here's the next step." Would it be feasible for you to speak up if you see this happening to people of color—men and women—in meetings?

_____

_____

_____

_____

_____

_____

Tightrope

Survey evidence shows that people of color get larger loads of office housework and less access to glamour work than white people do.[3] Is this a pattern you've noticed?

_____

_____

_____

_____

_____

If you notice that you get less office housework than someone else in your office does, we're not suggesting you volunteer to take some to even it out. But if you see one of your colleagues—especially one of color—constantly getting stuck with the office housework, could you have a conversation with them about it? For example, "Hey, I've noticed that you are often the one taking notes for the meetings. I know about a couple of strategies to avoid this pattern. Want to get coffee and talk through them?" (See strategies in chapter 13 of the workbook and pages 110–116 of *What Works*.)

_____

_____

_____

_____

_____

_____

As women at work, we all walk the same Tightrope between being seen as too feminine, so incompetent, or too masculine, so unliked. But racial bias can affect where on that Tightrope people think we should fall.

Different racial groups report differing pressures to behave in feminine ways. Black women are *less* likely to report pressures to behave in feminine ways (8 percent) than are Asian American women (61 percent), white women (36 percent), or Latinas (28 percent).

You may be under more pressure to behave in feminine ways than other women in your office are. Is this true for you?

_____

_____

_____

_____

_____

_____

If it is, how do you deal with that?

_____

_____

_____

_____

_____

One way that some women deal with such pressure is to shift it onto other women in the office by sending signals that other women should be more feminine as well. Have you noticed this in your office?

_____

_____

_____

_____

_____

_____

This is an example of how bias in the environment can translate into bias between women. Our advice? Don't go there. If you see another white woman in your office engage in this type of femininity policing, could you tell her to cut it out?

_____

_____

_____

_____

_____

Maternal Wall

Women from different racial groups may have different ideas about child care and family structures. For example, some women may view child care as a more communal process. Some may have different views about day care or about the role of family members and relatives in the child-rearing process. Some of these differences may be personal, and some may be influenced by race and culture.

Have you noticed that mothers in your office have different traditions and approaches to child care?

_____

_____

_____

_____

If so, do you notice that some of these differences might fall along racial lines?

_____

_____

_____

_____

_____

_____

Have you seen any conflicts or misunderstandings arise in the workplace that may be due to these differences in child-rearing approaches? For example, does conflict arise because one worker took time off work for a family emergency that another worker didn't consider an emergency?

_____

_____

_____

_____

_____

If different parenting practices have been a source of tension in your workplace, don't participate in it. Remember, there's no right way to be a mother. Criticizing other women for their practices or complaining about double standards if another mother takes more time off than you won't help your situation.

If you see moms sending messages to the other mothers in your office—particularly moms from a different race or culture—about the "right" way to mother, could you step in as an interrupter? We think calmly taking the mother aside and saying, "I know you meant well, but there is no one way to mother, and so-and-so might have a totally different perspective on how to parent than you do." Does that sound feasible?

_____

_____

_____

_____

_____

PART VII

Leave or Stay?

24

Sexual Harassment

📖 (Read with pages 75–79 of *What Works*)

Sexual harassment has been affecting women since probably the dawn of time. But until about the 1970s, it was seen as a bit of bad taste that any woman worth her salt could take care of privately.

Now, some things are illegal. Just so you know, here's what.

"Sleep with Me or You're Fired"

"Sleep with me or you're fired" is illegal. It's illegal to condition anything related to employment—hiring, firing, promotions, good assignments, anything—on having a sexual relationship.

Has this ever happened to you?

_____

_____

_____

_____

_____

_____

If it has, you've got two choices. One is to leave quietly. The other is to go to human resources (HR) and report it. Those are the only two choices. Why would you leave quietly? If you have no faith that anything effective will be done and that you will only end up leaving anyway—but with a bad reference.

Which did you do?

_____

_____

_____

_____

_____

_____

If you are in this situation and want to think through which option you should take, talk it through with someone *outside your organization*. Once you put someone inside your organization on notice of this kind of thing, they may consider themselves under a duty to report it—it's that illegal.

For a set of effective ways to defuse the situation if a work colleague has made a pass that you are most definitely not interested in, consult page 76 of *What Works*.

Porn on the Walls

It's also illegal to create a hostile environment based on sex. The classic case is one with porn on the walls where inappropriate comments abound.[1]

When does an unpleasant environment become "hostile"?

1. When the behavior is severe or pervasive.
2. When it would make a reasonable person uncomfortable.
3. When it has made *you* uncomfortable.

If it's really severe, it can only happen once. Bill Clinton reportedly once had a state trooper bring a state employee to his hotel room and exposed himself. If that actually happened, that's severe.[2] If it's not severe, the behavior has to be pervasive, which is a fancy word for this: it has to have happened more than once. How many times? Depends on how bad it is.

Do you feel like you face a hostile environment?

_____

_____

_____

_____

_____

_____

Note that you have to be able to prove that something made you uncomfortable. To do that, you have to let people know that the behavior is making you uncomfortable—that's also fair. You can't expect people to be mind readers. You can choose to let people know in whatever way makes most sense for you.

Have you tried saying, in an even tone, "This is making me uncomfortable"? If you haven't, that's the first step. If you have, what was the result?

_____

_____

_____

_____

_____

_____

If someone tries to shame you for *being* uncomfortable, just stand your ground with quiet conviction. How about, "Only I can tell what makes me uncomfortable, and this does."

Your Company's Sexual Harassment Policy

Even if behavior is not illegal, it may violate your company's sexual harassment policy. Almost every modern workplace has a sexual harassment policy. Does yours? If you don't know, find out. It might be in your company's employee handbook; look there first. If you can't find it, whom could you ask?

_____

_____

_____

_____

_____

_____

Your Experience

First, have you ever experienced something you define as sexual harassment, whether or not it fits the legal templates set out above?

_____

_____

_____

_____

_____

_____

How did you deal with it?

_____

_____

_____

_____

_____

What did a successful resolution look like to you, and did you get it? (For example, were you looking for a formal complaint to be lodged or for someone to get fired or to move to a different department to avoid that person?)

_____

_____

_____

_____

_____

_____

Why Do Men Sexually Harass Women?

The common thinking for why sexual harassment happens seems to be based on desire: men have desires for women, and they just can't help themselves sometimes.

We're compelled by another school of thought based on studies conducted by Jennifer Berdahl, who thinks that sexual harassment is motivated by power. Berdahl hypothesized that if sexual harassment stemmed solely from male desire, then feminine women would be harassed the most. But what she found was that more masculine-presenting women faced more severe harassment and that sexual harassment was more common in male-dominated workplaces than in female-dominated workplaces. From Berdahl: "sexual harassment is driven not out of desire for women who meet feminine ideals but out of a desire to punish those who violate them."[3]

Do you notice sexual harassment happening any more or any less to masculine-presenting women versus feminine-presenting women?

_____

_____

_____

_____

_____

_____

Is your workplace male or female dominated? If you have worked in both environments, have you noticed a difference in the level or frequency of sexual harassment?

_____

_____

_____

_____

_____

_____

Starting from Berdahl's school of thought, one function of sexual harassment may be to police women into a specific form of femininity. How does this apply to you? Have you ever felt this pressure?

_____

_____

_____

_____

_____

If there's sexual harassment in your workplace, sometimes it's driven by specific personalities in your office—one person or a small group of people. Is that the case in your office?

_____

_____

_____

_____

_____

_____

Other times, sexual harassment is institutional. For example, sometimes the office culture is built around "boys' clubs" that joke about sex and women's bodies to bond with each other. Sometimes groups of men in an office frequently go to bars to pick up women after work together or go to strip clubs together. Is that happening in your office?

_____

_____

_____

_____

_____

_____

If you're unsure, what are the ways that the men seem to bond in your office? Is there an exclusive "boys' club"? Do male friendships seem to be centered around work, their families, or something else?

_____

_____

_____

_____

_____

_____

Sometimes, it's not a specific group of men who drive this toxic culture; instead, it's more general. Sexual banter or sexual jokes can sometimes form the fabric of office bonding. Is this the case with your workplace? Here's a quick diagnostic test: to get in with the boss, do you have to tell a joke that involves reproductive body parts?

_____

_____

_____

_____

_____

_____

"She's a Sellout!" "She's a Prude!": How to Avoid Tug of War

Some women like dirty jokes. Some women have fun telling dirty jokes and find it funny and easy to bond with men through this kind of banter. Sometimes women who desire women find it easy to bond with the men who also desire women. Sometimes women grew up with brothers. Whatever the reason, is that you?

_____

_____

_____

_____

_____

Up to a point, there's not one rule about what is sexual harassment and what isn't when it comes to sexualized banter. It's a thin line, and every woman draws it differently. Some women enjoy it; some have no patience for it.

Be careful to avoid the Tug of War: judging other women for navigating these waters differently than you would or for being either too much one of the guys or not enough. Have you heard comments like, "Can you believe she said that?" or "Can you believe she went out with so-and-so last night?" Or "She's so uptight. Can't she take a joke?" Have you ever felt like that about someone else or heard someone talking about you that way?

_____

_____

_____

_____

_____

_____

If you've been talking like that, stop. As women, we have enough on our hands, navigating through the difficult minipolitics of everyday life, without making it harder for all of us by turning on each other. Women are different; there's nothing wrong with that. There's no need to get all judgy.

What If It's over the Line?

Again, it's important to remember that where each woman draws her line—what is acceptable, what is not—is her personal decision. It's often a matter of personal boundaries, and people differ. Where do you think your line is?

_____

_____

_____

_____

_____

If your line is different from that of other women in your office, it doesn't mean that your line is wrong or that anyone else's is either. Not liking dirty jokes doesn't make you a no-fun prude, and getting along with the guys' sexual banter doesn't make you a slut. The only thing that matters is whether you are comfortable with where you've drawn your line.

_____

_____

_____

_____

_____

What if you've been playing along with the guys quite comfortably, but then they go over the line? Has that ever happened to you?

_____

_____

_____

_____

_____

_____

Remember, just because Thing A was fine with you doesn't mean Thing B is as well. Refer to pages 75–79 of *What Works* for good ways to put your foot down when you need to.

Sexual Harassment of Women of Color

Some studies find that women of color report more sexual harassment than white women do.[4] Or they may experience sexual harassment that's different from that commonly experienced by white women, due to racial stereotypes being triggered.

For black women, sexual harassment sometimes stems from stereotypes about women as sexually available or voracious—stereotypes that are particularly prevalent with regard to black women dating back to slavery.

Asian American women sometimes face expectations that they will play the role of the exotic Oriental or the passive sex object.

Latina women may face sexual harassment due to the stereotypes that they are "vivacious" or because they may dress differently from other women in the workplace (see chapter 22 in the Workbook). (Note to Future Self: Change all of this. Forever. Figure out how to erase negative racial stereotypes from human consciousness. If that can't happen, make sure this doesn't happen in your workplace.)

25

Knowing When to Leave Your Job

📖 (Read with pages 261–273 of *What Works*)

Through this workbook, you've learned tips, strategies, and exercises to help you get to the position in your company that you deserve—whether it's a promotion, a more flexible work schedule, more challenging projects, or just better recognition of your work from your colleagues. We hope that by using these tools, your work life will improve.

But what if those tools don't work? Or what if you don't feel motivated to expend a ton of your energy trying to make your current workplace a better environment?

Maybe it's time to leave. If you can't improve your situation or feel too checked out to try, you may be ready to pursue your next venture. This is a big decision, one that requires thoughtful deliberation and strategic planning. This chapter will help you decide if it's the right time for you to leave.

Sign #1: You're Undervalued

Take a moment and write down the last three times you felt valued at your job by your co-workers and superiors. This could be anything, from direct praise from a boss ("Great job on that report, Pam. You nailed it.") or a time when one of your ideas got implemented into a new project or initiative or a time when a supervisor consulted you in a respectful way.

1. _____

_____

2. _____

_____

3. _____

_____

Review what you just wrote. Are all three spaces blank? Are all three times from the past six months, or are they from years past? Did they spring to your mind easily, or did you struggle to remember them?

_____

_____

_____

_____

_____

_____

   Now think about how you feel looking at them. Are you reminded why you took this job in the first place? Do they feel fulfilling or pale in comparison to your frustrations with the job?

_____

_____

_____

_____

_____

_____

   Loyalty to your job is valuable but only if you get rewarded appropriately for it. Do you feel you've gotten appropriately rewarded for your loyalty?

_____

_____

_____

_____

_____

_____

   Think about the future at your current job. Are you excited about the prospects of moving up in your company? Do you expect to be promoted within the next one to three years? (A reasonable time for promotion depends on your company and your seniority level. It may be longer than that.)

_____

_____

_____

_____

_____

_____

If you don't expect to be promoted, analyze why that is. Sometimes it's just because you're at a comfortable position that suits your skills and needs well and lets you and your family live comfortably. There's no shame in that. Is that the case?

_____

_____

_____

_____

_____

_____

Now it's time to see whether gender bias may be playing a role. Look around you. Does it seem that women have to prove themselves more than men do to be promoted? Note that sometimes women get the next job—but not the job title or salary that goes with it. Is any of that happening? If so, Prove-It-Again! bias may be affecting women's advancement at your organization.

_____

_____

_____

_____

_____

_____

Now take a look back to chapter 13 in the Workbook to help you understand whether there's a fair allocation of glamour work and office housework that's affecting your ability to gain the skills and experiences that make you ready for promotion.

Or maybe things were going great until you had children, and then, suddenly, promotions stopped abruptly—not only for you but for a lot of the other mothers at your organization.

Or another possibility, as you look above you, do you feel your organization has already filled its "woman slot," and you can't see another one opening up?

Is any of that happening?

_____

_____

_____

_____

_____

_____

If any of these patterns is pervasive, it may be time to think about moving on.

Or ask yourself the simple question: "How many times have I been passed over for advancement?"

_____

_____

If the answer is one or two, keep reading the chapter. If the answer is three or more, consider putting this book down and quitting right now. (Just kidding. Go read the next chapter in the workbook, "How to Leave Your Job without Burning Bridges," first. Then quit.)

Sign #2: There Aren't Many Women at the Senior Levels of the Company

Who succeeds at your company? How many women are in positions of seniority at your company?

_____

Were there many women at the top, but they left within short periods of each other?

_____

If there are no women (or very few) at senior levels in your company, that could be a red flag. As we've discussed, there are multiple reasons why women get passed over for promotion, partnership, and leadership. Whatever the reason is, you can be pretty sure that it is *not* because there simply aren't qualified women to fill those roles. If your company has a history of passing over women for promotion, it is likely that this policy probably will not change with you, barring a serious attitude adjustment inside the company.

If there are women at senior levels in your company, think of two or three whom you admire and aspire to be like professionally. After identifying your models, try to find out a little more information about their path by talking to them. How long did it take for them to get there? If they have children, was the process of taking leave and returning relatively smooth, or did they have to fight to get their position back? Do they feel valued in their senior position, or do they face the same obstacles that you do, only with a different title? Write down your findings below:

1. _____

_____

_____

_____

_____

_____

2. _____

_____

_____

_____

_____

_____

3. _____

_____

_____

_____

_____

_____

After talking with senior women at your company and reviewing their answers, do you feel more hopeful about your future at your company? Were you able to identify specific steps these women took to reach where they are now that you could mirror? Or do the sacrifices and struggles your models face sound like more of the slog that you've been dealing with? Jot down your thoughts:

_____

_____

_____

_____

_____

Some women thrive in work environments where advancing higher is a challenge. If you are one of those women who look at an all-male leadership board and think, "That's all gonna change with me," then go for it, and more power to you! If you're not and can't find a couple of good examples of female leadership at your company to model yourself after, then it may be time to find a more diverse working environment. After all, studies show that diverse companies perform better. So relocating to a less homogeneous company may be good not just for your mental sanity but also for your career and your bank account.[1]

Sign #3: You Can Move Up Elsewhere

"If you want to move up, you've got to move." This is true more often than it should be.

An important piece of research that professional women should know is that it can be more beneficial for women to change jobs rather than to stay at the same company and work their way up. One study found that for highly educated women, the return on experience brought from prior jobs is significantly higher than for men, about 40 percent.[2] This suggests that professional women should always keep an eye out for opportunities outside their company, even if the job they currently have is still working well.

This doesn't mean that you should change jobs every six months. Obviously there is a risk in appearing flighty to your prospective employers, and you could lose out on the experience of building meaningful long-term relationships with co-workers and/or your client base.

Take a moment and go over your resume, either on paper or just your mental resume, and analyze your position.

Are you in the first year of your job?

_____

Have you had more than two jobs in the past five years?

_____

Does your line of work depend on long-term relationships with clients or on a solid network?

_____

If you answered yes to these questions, then exercise caution in moving jobs too quickly. There can be value in making a name for yourself in a certain company in a certain city. (That said, if you're miserable and see a better opportunity elsewhere, go for it! Nothing is a sure bet.)

If your resume has fewer previous jobs than skills, there may be more benefits to looking elsewhere for promotion than staying put. Remember though, if moving jobs, always move up. Avoid making a lateral move. Studies show that women, more than men, are financially penalized following a move and on average have to work for three more years to attain the salary they had before their move.[3] With that in mind, try to find a job that is at a higher level and that pays you more.

Are you in a position to move up elsewhere? Spend a few minutes mapping out higher-level jobs that you could take at different organizations:

_____

_____

_____

_____

_____

_____

Even if you're not sure, it doesn't hurt to look! Looking for another job while you still have this one can

- ✓ Help build confidence
- ✓ Help you decide whether the job you have is a good fit
- ✓ Give you an idea about whether it will be easy to move up

Sign #4: You've Exhausted Your Options (or Yourself)

If you're considering leaving your job but find yourself thinking, "Am I sure I did everything I could to try and make this job work for me?" then this exercise is for you.

Have you . . .

_____ **1.** Talked to someone about it?

If you haven't yet directly gone to your boss and asked for exactly what you want, do it right now. Asking for something outright doesn't always get you exactly what you wanted, but it often helps. At the least, it lets your boss know that you are ready for a new challenge.

If you have spoken with your superiors about the bias you feel at work, about the promotion you got passed over for, about the raise you were scheduled to receive but didn't, and it fell on deaf ears, then move along to number 2. At least you tried.

_____*2.* Considered that it's just a rough patch?

No one should stick with a job that makes them miserable if they don't want to. But before taking the big step of leaving your job, it's worth it to consider how long you've been unhappy for and if there are any short-term causes. For example, if you got stuck with a big project that you find totally uninspiring, you may feel like finding a different job. But if the project will wrap up within the next few months, it may be worth it to stick it out.

Sometimes giving yourself a time frame helps. Say, "If I'm still this unhappy in three months, I'll start job hunting," or "If I haven't been given a project that's career enhancing by Christmas, I'll quit."

_____*3.* Tried transferring within your company?

If a major source of your unhappiness at work comes from a specific person, then perhaps looking into moving laterally within your company would be a wise move. In large organizations, moving employees around is a common solution to internal conflicts. If you generally like your company but have gotten stuck in a toxic pattern with an individual or small group of people, then moving to a different branch might help you personally while not hurting you professionally.

_____*4.* Thought about your formal options?

Sometimes, if the patterns of bias you face at work are severe, you may choose to file an internal complaint or take legal action. Pursuing these options is tricky, and even if you don't decide to go through with it, you should still be aware of your legal rights to do so. Spend some time researching your company's policies with internal complaint procedure, as well as legal processes for discrimination claims. A good place to start is by reading pages 268–271 of *What Works*, which will give you an overview of your options and some recommendations for starting the process.

If you have tried any or all of these techniques and your work situation has not improved, it may be time to consider moving on. Again, loyalty is important, and trying to fix your current situation before finding a new one can be beneficial. But loyalty without return just makes you miserable. (Note to Future Self: Reward loyalty with cupcakes. And raises. Maybe both.)

Sign #5: You Hate Your Job

Though it may sound obvious, sometimes it's not always clear to ourselves when something is making us miserable. Sometimes we get so caught up in the grind of our jobs that we don't realize the toll it's taking on us. Have you ever gotten out of a relationship only to look back and think, "That person was a total loser. I can't believe I sacrificed my X, Y, Z for them." Your job should be something you enjoy, not something you suffer through because you feel you have to.

Thinking about your job, what are the top-five things you like about it:

1. _____

_____

2. _____

_____

3. _____

_____

4. _____

_____

5. _____

_____

Look at your list and pick the three things you would miss the most about your job if you were to leave. In the space below, write down whether these are things you can find at a different job somewhere else or whether they are unique to your particular current job:

1. _____

_____

2. _____

_____

3. _____

_____

Now write out the five things about your job you dislike the most:

1. _____

_____

2. _____

_____

3. _____

_____

_4._ _____

_____

_5._ _____

_____

Look at your list and try to think about each item in terms of its problem: is it inside you or outside you? For example, if you wrote, "My boss is sexist and doesn't respect my ideas," that's obviously a problem that is outside your control. If you wrote, "I hate all my co-workers," that may have more to do with you than with everyone else. (Of course, it's always possible that all of your co-workers are the worst—but maybe unlikely.)

Categorize each item on your list as "inside" or "outside" (some may be a little of both; in that case, write "both"):

_1._ _____

_2._ _____

_3._ _____

_4._ _____

_5._ _____

Does your list of things you dislike about your job have more to do with problems inside you or outside you?

_____

_____

Obviously, no job is going to be fun and roses all the time. But in general, the times when work makes you miserable should be far less and last for shorter amounts of time than the times when work makes you feel fulfilled.

If it sounds helpful, figure out for yourself what your personal limit on work-related misery is (that is, what percentage of your time you are willing to let your job negatively affect you): 15 percent of the time? 20 percent of the time? Write your answer here:

_____

Then check in with yourself once every evening for two weeks. Ask yourself how your workday was:

_____ Great!

_____ Generally fine

_____ Exhausting but worth it

_____ Not great, but maybe tomorrow will be better

_____ Terrible

	Monday	Tuesday	Wednesday	Thursday	Friday	Saturday	Sunday
Week 1							
Week 2							

If you answer "terrible" more than three or four times in a two-week period, you might hate your job.

Finally, if you're still not sure whether you want to leave your job, do what one New Girl recommends: put both options, leave or stay, into a hat. If you pick out option "stay" and feel disappointed (or nauseous), then you know it's time to leave.

26

How to Leave Your Job without Burning Bridges

Congratulations! If you're reading this section for advice on how to leave your job, then you've already done the most important part: you've made a decision. Leaving your job is never an easy option, but languishing over the decision for too long can make you crazy. Whatever the factors involved, you've analyzed them, weighed them, and debated them. Now stop thinking about them.

Is Today the Day?

The first step to leaving your job is figuring out whether you need to wait to have another job lined up before you quit. This depends both on your financial situation and on your ability to continue tolerating your current job.

First, your financial situation: if you were to quit tomorrow, how long could you be unemployed before you or your family started to panic?

_____

_____

_____

_____

_____

_____

Is that enough time for you to find another job? Compare it to the time it took to find your current job:

_____

_____

_____

_____

_____

_____

Make sure you're factoring in the following:
Will you collect any money for unused vacation days?

_____

_____

Will you get any retirement fund money back when you quit?

_____

_____

Will you get a tax return anytime soon?

_____

_____

If you have a partner, do they have any bonuses or cash infusions coming soon?

_____

_____

Are there any big expenses coming up in your future, such as a kid needing braces, a car that's on its last legs, or a school tuition payment that's due? It might be worth waiting until the calendar looks relatively big-payment free.

_____

_____

_____

_____

_____

_____

_____

_____

One New Girl we talked to used her exit to negotiate a severance package. She stayed at a job longer than she wanted to, until her company paid her to go: "It's not like I was incompetent or anything like that. They weren't firing me for cause. They needed to offer me a package to leave, to just move on."[1]

Have you heard of other people being offered severance packages in your company? If not, ask around and see if you can discreetly gather some intelligence.

_____

_____

_____

If waiting for a severance package sounds like a realistic idea for you, make sure you have some emotional guards ready. Set yourself a limit on how long you're willing to stay at this job—one month? six months? Remember, it's possible your bosses won't ever offer you the package you hope for.

What's your limit?

_____

It might also be helpful to line up a friend or co-worker you can call when you can't remember why you're staying at a job you hate. That way, when you're feeling like quitting mid-Monday morning, they can remind you why you're still there: you're waiting for them to pay you to leave.

List three people you can call when you need the extra encouragement:

1. _____

2. _____

3. _____

Making Your Graceful Exit

As much as you may (or may not) want to, it is always a good idea to leave a job respectfully and in good standing. You never know when the people at your work will pop up again in your life, and you don't want to screw your future self over before you've even started.

Plus, it will make you feel better. So this job wasn't your dream job, and maybe it was really crappy at times. But you still tried your best, put your all into it, and deserve to leave feeling like it was worthwhile.

If you need to get it out of your system, go watch *Office Space* and then go hit some tennis balls or whatever you need to do to relax.

Step 1: Give Them Enough Time

This may sound like a no-brainer, but exiting gracefully relies on your employer not feeling like you're leaving it high and dry. The basic question to ask yourself is, "How long will it take my company to replace me?"

If you're in a service-industry position or most nondirectorial positions, the two-week period of notice is traditional.

If you're in a specialized position or high up in your organization, it may be expected and respectful to offer more than two weeks to find your replacement.

Where does your job fall?

_____

_____

If you're not sure about how much notice you should give, try thinking back to a time when someone in your organization in a comparable position left in good standing. How much time did they give? If you're not sure, could you ask them?

_____

_____

If you're not able to ask them, reach out to your network. Someone a little more senior in a similar type of company would be ideal. You could say, "I'm considering leaving my job to pursue opportunities elsewhere, and I'm not sure how much notice I should give my company. What is the amount of notice you expect from your employees?" Write down your findings here:

_____

_____

_____

_____

_____

_____

Once you've identified how much notice to give, plan how you're going to do it.

We highly recommend doing this in person. It is a little scarier; but it will give you the chance to explain, and it will give your employer the chance to ask questions and maybe beg you to stay by offering you the moon (and stars)? Furthermore, if your boss wakes up to an "I'm leaving" e-mail from you, it may make them upset, and you don't want to give them the opportunity to bad-mouth you to other people.

If you're convinced, set up a meeting with your boss. Don't tell them explicitly what it's about. Go with the old "I'd like to discuss a couple of things with you."

If you're worried the meeting won't go well, try working out your strategy with someone you trust—someone with good judgment. Who might that be?

_____

_____

If there are structural impediments to an in-person meeting (you work remotely, your boss is traveling, etc.), then try and schedule a phone call. While not as good as in-person, a phone call still allows for a dialogue to happen. An e-mail (or, God forbid, a text) can be taken the wrong way, can be misconstrued, and you won't have any idea as to how your boss reacts.

Step 2: Be Honest (Enough)

Like breaking up with someone, it always feels easier to go the "it's not you, it's me" route when explaining to your boss why you're leaving (especially for women, as we've discussed). While this may feel easier, you want to avoid feeling regretful later on ("I wish I had told them that I would have stayed if they had given me the chance to do X"). Also, the reason why you're leaving is super-valuable feedback for your employer to have, and if they are a decent boss, they will appreciate the information.

Usually, the reason why you're leaving is a little bit because of you and a little bit because of your environment. Let's figure out how to convey why you're leaving in an honest way that won't hurt you or your employer.

Write down the main reason(s) why you're leaving your job:

_____

_____

_____

_____

_____

If you wrote down something like "I can get a better job elsewhere" or "No opportunities for advancement," try recrafting your reasons in a more diplomatic way. For example, "I feel like I learned a lot at this job and got some great opportunities. But this new job will allow me to develop X or Y skills, to build on the foundation I've established during my time here."

Now you try:

_____

_____

_____

_____

_____

_____

If you're reasons for leaving are more targeted at the specific organization—"I can't stand my boss"; "The culture is toxic to my happiness"—consider softening the information while still delivering the feedback (another example of gender judo): "I try not to let personalities affect me at the workplace. Unfortunately, the personality conflicts that I have been facing have negatively affected my ability to be as productive and engaged as I want to be. Though I tried X, Y, and Z to find a solution to these problems, they have persisted. So I think it's time for me to move on, before it negatively affects the company."

Now you try:

_____

_____

_____

_____

_____

_____

Finally, if your reasons for leaving the company have to do with work-life balance issues, make sure not to make yourself the martyr and also not to take all the blame for why it didn't work out. If your company expects 24-hour on-call employees or doesn't accommodate employees also being parents/siblings/caregivers, then it is not your personality flaw that is making you leave. The company may have unsustainable expectations of their employees, and they will continue to hemorrhage talent. It serves both you and your company to bring it up.

Try something like, "I have really enjoyed putting so much energy, passion, and hard work into this position. When I was single / childless / without caregiving responsibilities, it was fun to stay up late with everyone to finish a project / brainstorm new initiatives / etc. However, as my life became more full, it became more challenging to devote more than X hours a day to my job, without the room to change my schedule. I tried X, Y, and Z to accommodate my personal responsibilities while still being dedicated to my job, but the value placed on being a 24-hour employee persisted. One of my priorities is to have a career that also fits with my life, so I need to pursue a job elsewhere that gives me the flexibility to do so."

Now you try:

_____

_____

_____

_____

_____

_____

You get the gist: Remind them that you have been a good employee who enjoyed your job. Explain to them the problem in direct but vague terms. Outline steps you have taken in the past to fix it on your own. This leads you easily to the conclusion that you have to leave.

If your reason for leaving wasn't addressed above, try writing it out with this model:

_____

_____

_____

_____

_____

_____

Step 3: Consider Your Network

Before you step out the door and breathe in the sweet air of new beginnings, consider making an effort to keep some of your connections at work. Think about your network and if there are folks you would like to have in your court in the long term.

Chances are, shortly after you tell your boss you're leaving, everyone else in your department/company will know, too. This is the law of gossip—it travels fast. Is there anyone at your organization you like, who you think would be valuable to maintain a relationship with? Even if you haven't been particularly close to them, your exiting opens up the possibility for a new manner of relationship.

Write down the people (if any) whom you'd like to maintain contact with:

1. _____

2. _____

3. _____

4. _____

5. _____

Once you've identified them, figure out the best way to reach out to them. This will depend on how much time you have as well as the logistics of your organization.

Here are some ideas:

✓ Send an e-mail: "Hi, X. You may have heard that this is my last week with the company. I just wanted you to know that I have really enjoyed working with you / learning from you / getting to know you / watching you lead this initiative / etc. I'd love to stay in touch and hear about how your project winds up / how the case settles / etc. Here's my personal e-mail / cell phone." (Note, make sure to follow up! See chapter 10 in the workbook for tips.)

✓ Ask them out to coffee / lunch / brunch / book club.

✓ Friend them on social media. (This can also signal, "Hey, I want to be friends! Not just work acquaintances!")

If you have clients, should you tell them? This is a sticky issue that will vary tremendously depending on the type of work you do, where you're leaving to (i.e., a competing organization or something different), the temperament of your boss, and your relationship with them. That being said, we think there are a few basic tenets you could consider.

1. If you worked closely with someone, especially over a long period of time, you don't want to let them find out that you're leaving from an "Out of Office" message. Even if you didn't work with them super closely but want to maintain a relationship, add them to the list you made above of people to send out a message to let them know that you're leaving your company and a way to contact you.

2. If you have clients and want to let them know that you're leaving, make sure the message you send is extremely gracious and open-ended. *No* trash-talking your current job, no matter how worthy of trash talk it is. Try something like, "I just want you to know that I've accepted a role at _____. It's been wonderful working with you. Here is my personal e-mail so we can stay in touch." Make it short and sweet, so no one can accuse you of stealing clients.

3. If you have a good relationship with your boss, consider talking to them about this. You may want to give your clients someone to contact at the organization that you're leaving. In some cases, it may make the most sense for your boss to send out an e-mail to your client list and let them know that you're leaving. This would show that you're a true professional: able to maintain good working relationships through tricky situations. Then you could follow up with your clients afterward and let them know that you enjoyed working with them and "hey, just in case, here's my e-mail."

Step 4: Transition Purposefully

Transitioning out of a job can be an eerie time, especially if you've been at the job for many years and have invested a lot of yourself into it. Training your replacement, clearing out your desk, saying good-bye to the coffee shop next door can all bring up bittersweet emotions (sometimes existential terror).

Do yourself a favor: be prepared.

How do you feel about the prospect of transitioning out of your job?

_____

_____

_____

_____

_____

_____

What are the things that will be hard to say good-bye to?

_____

_____

_____

_____

_____

_____

What are your worst fears with leaving this job?

_____

_____

_____

_____

_____

_____

Now that those are out in the open, you can be ready for them. If while cleaning out your desk you start to panic that you made the wrong choice, remember that your feelings are normal, but they aren't real.

If helpful, fill out this cheat sheet now so that you can look at it if you start to freak out while transitioning:

Reasons I'm leaving my job:

1. _____

2. _____

3. _____

Why I'm going to be just fine without this job:

1. _____

2. _____

3. _____

Things I'm looking forward to doing after I leave this job:

1. _____

2. _____

3. _____

Remember, don't get too hung up on what you've enjoyed about this job. In your new job, you'll enjoy different things. Don't just focus on what you're *losing*. Look forward to all the good stuff that's about to happen! You know that barista at the corner who always congratulates you when you buy a bacon donut on your consumption of "vitamin H" (happiness)? There's someone equally awesome awaiting you near your next job.

Being generous with your time and expertise during your transition will help ensure the gracefulness of your exit. While it may be tempting to check out and say "Figure it out, losers!" your bosses will be calmed and grateful if they see you making sure everything is handed off properly.

If you're training your replacement, try to be as neutral and job focused as possible. Don't pass off your issues and injuries onto the next person in your position. Remember, they are probably very excited to have your job! Don't ruin it for them.

If you're not training your replacement, try to invest some serious time into your transition memo or whatever the equivalent at your job is. Not only will it help the person stepping in, but it gives you a last opportunity to show everyone how much you have been doing over the years and what an asset you are. It never hurts to make a good last impression.

PART VIII

The Final Touches

27

Work-Life Balance

What work-life balance means is different for everyone, but one thing's for sure: if you don't have a balance that works for you, you'll probably be a lot less committed to your job and certainly will be a lot less happy than if you do.

How much time you spend on leisure activities is a strong predictor of life satisfaction.[1] Don't give up before you start. Joan was really grumpy about her work-life balance a few years ago and was complaining about it to a friend. The friend wisely challenged her to get her act together and make some changes. One thing Joan noticed is that it is really, really important to her to have 15 minutes a day to read the paper. *15 minutes.* She reorganized her mornings and now takes half an hour to read the paper and eat a leisurely breakfast. She's much happier.

For Marina, making time for leisure reading is important. Reading bad detective novels and mystery books is a way for her to relax and decompress. She realized that when work got really busy, she stopped making time to read and felt guilty when she read for fun: "Isn't there something more useful I could be doing?" She decided to make a rule: during her 20-minute bus ride to work, she would not check her e-mail or think about work. Instead, she would read a chapter of her leisure book. It's only 20 minutes, but it made a huge difference.

An Experiment: Your Work-Life Balance Plan

So here's where to start. List here five things that you're too busy to do that you would be happier if you did regularly.

1. _____

   _____

2. _____

   _____

3. _____

   _____

4. _____

   _____

5. _____

_____

You're going to run an experiment on your life. It will take a month. Now take the one thing you listed above that's the easiest to change. What is that one?

_____

_____

How could you change that? For example, Joan just reset in her own mind when she wanted to get down to work—a half an hour later than she had been doing. Since that may not be possible for everyone, how could you rearrange your life so that you get to do just one thing that would make you feel happier and more balanced?

_____

_____

_____

_____

_____

_____

Okay, now do that for one week before you read further in this chapter. If for some reason a crisis arises—it's all hands on deck at work, and you can't fulfill your resolution this week—then begin next week.

Now go back to your list. What's the next easiest thing to accomplish? How could you change that?

_____

_____

_____

_____

_____

Now do that for one week while maintaining your first change. Was that feasible? What did you have to change?

_____

_____

_____

_____

_____

_____

Keep on moving down your list.
Thing 3 I would love to change:

_____

_____

_____

_____

_____

Thing 4:

_____

_____

_____

_____

_____

Thing 5:

_____

_____

_____

_____

_____

Reflect. How far down your list did you get?

_____

How much time away from work does that translate into?

_____

_____

_____

_____

_____

_____

Is that sustainable?

_____

_____

_____

_____

_____

Working harder and taking more flak than your male peers gets exhausting and can lead you to burn out quickly. Don't work so hard that you have to quit your job to keep your sanity.

Work-Life Balance Rx

Now that you've identified the five things that are most important to your sense of balance, you're ready for the advanced course: Work-Life Balance Rx.

Given that women often find that they have to prove themselves more than men do, it's important not to burn out.

Focus on what you can do outside work that makes you feel whole. Pick something in each of the categories below that you enjoy or particularly appeals to you and then make a resolution about it. It should be something small and manageable, so that you can really enjoy it without feeling like it's just another thing on your to-do list—something like "take a bubble bath once a week" or "make a dinner date with an old friend."

Physical activity (e.g., "run a 5K," "go to two yoga classes a week," "walk at least 10,000 steps a day"):

_____

_____

Doing physical activity naturally decreases stress and depression.[2] Even five minutes of exercise can help. And, of course, then you can eat more. If you love to eat as much as we do, that in itself is a reason to exercise!

Social time (e.g., "read to the kids for 20 minutes before bed twice a week," "call Mom on Sunday afternoons," "go on a Tinder date"):

_____

_____

Entertainment (e.g., "start a mystery novel," "go see a movie," "catch up on *New Girl*"):

_____

_____

Hobby time (e.g., "learn to bake bread," "practice guitar twice a week," "knit a scarf"):

_____

_____

"Me" time (e.g., "take a long bath once a week," "take a week of vacation time," "meditate for five minutes a day"):

_____

_____

Now here's the really hard part: sometimes you're going to get so busy that you're going to have to take a break from these activities. That's fine and even necessary. Just don't let a break turn into a breakup. Come back to this list, add to it, cross stuff off, and always remember that investing in your personal fulfillment is an important part of investing in your career.

What If Your Work's Eating Up Your Life and There's Not a Thing You Can Do about It?

This happens. The first question is, is it temporary or permanent? Think over the past four weeks. Did you have the work-life balance you want?

If not, why not? Was the imbalance the result of something temporary or permanent or somewhere in between?

_____

_____

_____

_____

_____

If it was temporary, explain here when it will end:

_____

_____

_____

_____

_____

Go back to your Work-Life Balance Plan. What are the least time-intensive elements of that? Could you implement them to get you through?

_____

_____

_____

_____

_____

If the imbalance is permanent, is the job worth it? Sometimes it's important, particularly at the start of your career, to compromise on your sense of balance in order to secure a crucial opportunity. Is that true of you now? If so, how long will you have to put up with this in order to secure that opportunity? Is it worth it to you? (If you don't know how long, instead write about how long you are willing to wait.)

_____

_____

_____

_____

_____

Remember, it's your life. Even if you enjoy your work a lot, chances are there are a lot of other things you enjoy, too. If you are not getting time to do them, then there's something off about your life plan. As the saying goes, you can always get another job. You can't get another life.

28

Don't Worry, Be Happy

Being miserable is a bad career move for many reasons. If you are miserable because you work all the time, that lack of balance can lead to poor health and burnout. If you are miserable because you catastrophize, this can cause people to question whether you have good judgment. Being miserable because you worship the hole in the donut can cause you to be reluctant to take the kinds of risks that make for an interesting, challenging career.

We're not talking about being inanely optimistic. We're talking about being willing to think positive while being realistic. This chapter will provide some basic tools, based on the comparatively new field of positive psychology.[1] Psychology traditionally studied what happens when things go awry; positive psychology studies what happens when things go well.

People who score high in positivity are more likely to like their jobs, more likely to be married, and more likely to have happy marriages—and studies that follow people over time suggest that positive affect foreshadows happiness in these domains rather than simply reflecting it.[2]

You Can Control How Happy You Are: Gratitude, Optimism, Grit

It will come as no surprise that being employed and how often you have sex are correlated with how happy you are. Other factors are more surprising, notably gratitude, optimism, and self-esteem.

You can't control a lot of things in life, but you can control how grateful you feel for the things that have gone right for you. One way to develop gratitude is to write an annual "gratitude letter" to someone who did something you are grateful for during the past year.

You also can control how optimistic you are. Mindless optimism won't help.[3] The key is to be optimistic about things you can potentially change but not about those you can't.[4] This summarizes the Serenity Prayer: "God grant me the serenity to accept the things I cannot change, the courage to change those I can, and the wisdom to know the difference."

Or, if you prefer musicals, Joan quotes the words to "Happy Talk" from *South Pacific*: "You got to have a dream; if you don't have a dream, how're you gonna have a dream come true?"

A more scientific way to put this is to say that you should draw positive inferences in the absence of evidence where doing so will be motivating for you. There's no point in engaging in anticipatory regret. There'll be time enough for that if things don't work out.

Think of a time when an outcome you really cared about was unclear. What's the most pessimistic version of what could have happened?

_____

_____

_____

_____

_____

What's the most optimistic version?

_____

_____

_____

_____

_____

Get in the habit, after a reality check, of drawing positive inferences in a context where positive thinking might change the outcome. What the research shows is that it is useful to be optimistic in contexts where hope can affect the outcome.

Grit is "perseverance and passion for long-term goals."[5] Grit is the ability to persevere even in the face of setbacks.

Remember this: behind every successful person is a string of failures.

Every accomplished person became successful because they did not let their failures dissuade them from continuing to pursue their goals. Obviously, it's easier to have grit if you choose to embrace the heroic assumption that things will work out if you just keep with it. Optimism makes grit easier.

What's an example of a personal or professional setback that mattered a lot to you?

_____

_____

_____

_____

_____

_____

How did you overcome it?

_____

_____

_____

_____

_____

Did you exhibit grit and optimism? If so, how? If not, how could you have done so? Might it have made a difference or made you less miserable even if things did not ultimately work out?

_____

_____

_____

_____

_____

So work on your gratitude, optimism, and grit. And remember that some things many of us feel a lot of angst about—income, intelligence, physical attractiveness, having children—don't correlate with happiness.

"Have a Good Day" Exercise

What does it mean to have a good day? Something different for everyone. Do you know what it means for you? To find out, try this. Every day for between two and four weeks, write down all your major activities. At the end of each day, rate how good or bad your day was, from 1 to 10, with 1 being stupendous, 4 average, and 10 terrible, horrible, no good, very bad day.

	Monday	Tuesday	Wednesday	Thursday	Friday	Saturday	Sunday
	Activity	Activity	Activity	Activity	Activity	Activity	Activity
6 a.m.							
7 a.m.							
8 a.m.							
9 a.m.							
10 a.m.							
11 a.m.							
12 p.m.							
1 p.m.							
2 p.m.							
3 p.m.							
4 p.m.							
5 p.m.							
6 p.m.							
7 p.m.							
8 p.m.							
9 p.m.							
10 p.m.							
11 p.m.							
12 a.m.							
	Overall rating:	Overall rating:	Overall rating:	Overall rating:	Overall rating:	Overall Rating:	Overall rating:

Now look back at your sheet. What do you notice about your good days?

_____

_____

_____

_____

What do you notice about your bad days?

_____

_____

_____

_____

_____

What are small steps you could take to make more days good days?

_____

_____

_____

_____

_____

Are you having consistently bad days? If so, is it a matter of "wait, and this too shall pass," or is this an indicator that you need to make some large changes in your life? (If it's your job that's bumming you out, turn to part 7, "Leave or Stay?")

_____

_____

_____

_____

_____

If you need to make some large changes, what's the first step you could take to begin that process? Just the first step, which will often be reaching out to someone you can trust who can provide a reality check to see whether things are as bad as they seem.

_____

_____

_____

_____

_____

Often people find that by taking relatively small steps, they can sharply increase their proportion of good days. Joan does this exercise with the students in her leadership class every year. Two things typically jump out:

1. Many people notice that a good day is one when they have exercised. Exercise has been documented to increase not only physical health but also mental health.[6] Do you exercise regularly?

_____

_____

_____

_____

_____

If you don't, is now the time to start? Marina, after hearing Joan's students describe how much better they felt on days when they exercised, tried to remember the last time she exercised (read: never). But hearing those testimonials pushed her to start. Now exercise is a regular part of her life, after having spent the first 26 years vehemently avoiding it.

What's the best way to ensure that you do exercise? And how many times a week would be ideal? For many people, the best approach is to slot exercise into their schedule at specific times a week. Another good strategy is to make a date to exercise regularly with someone else. Marina found that she needed a carrot to get her to exercise at first, which she found in the form of watching bad TV on her phone while using the elliptical ("I can only watch *KUWTK* if I go to the gym"). Use this space to jot down how you are going to make sure you get enough exercise:

_____

_____

_____

_____

2. The other thing that jumps out is that, for many people, spending time with family and friends is key to having a good day. Is that true of you?

_____

_____

_____

_____

_____

If so, how much time? Use this space to jot down how you are going to make sure you make time for family and friends:

_____

_____

_____

_____

_____

What if you are an introvert? That means that you get energy from being alone, rather than from being with people. The opposite is true of an extrovert. If you are an introvert, you may still enjoy spending time with people, but it's also important for you to take enough time to be quiet and alone. (A great read: *Quiet: The Power of Introverts in a World That Can't Stop Talking*, by Susan Cain—highly recommended for introverts.) Are you an introvert or an extrovert?

_____

_____

_____

_____

_____

If you need to recharge by spending time alone, use this space to jot down how you will carve out that time:

_____

_____

_____

_____

_____

_____

"Three Good Things" Exercise

Human beings are wired to have better recall of bad things than good things. Again, a simple exercise can help. Every day for a month, at dinner or before you go to sleep, take time to write down three good things that happened to you that day.[7] They can be large or small things, from drinking a new flavor of kombucha to a marriage proposal. After each thing, write a sentence or two about why the good thing happened ("He knows I love ice cream. When he bought it, he must have been thinking about me."). When one of the founders of positive psychology, Martin Seligman, did this exercise with his students, 60 percent reported that they were still counting their blessings six months later.[8]

Here's a form to help you:

	Monday	Tuesday	Wednesday	Thursday	Friday	Saturday	Sunday
1st good thing							
2nd good thing							
3rd good thing							

It's also a great tradition to establish at the dinner table: go around and share one good thing that happened to you today. It's great modeling for your kids. (Note that this doesn't mean you should discourage yourself, or anyone else, from processing the bad stuff that happens, too!)

And here's a helpful hint: make a habit of stopping on an up note, even if it means you stop a bit early or rearrange the order of tasks. If you end on a peak, that will color your memory of the whole day.[9]

Build on Your Strengths

The American educational and employment systems tend to focus on weaknesses: how to identify them and how to correct them. In fact, what's far more important are your strengths.

Think about it. If you work really, really hard on your weaknesses, you might bring those skills up to average. But if you design your work life to tap your strengths, you will be bringing your best self to work.

Ask a close friend, someone you trust and respect and who knows you well, to tell a story about when you were your best self. Recount the story here:

_____

_____

_____

_____

_____

_____

Were you surprised, or did the story pretty much reflect your self-image?

_____

_____

_____

_____

_____

_____

If you were surprised, how did the story change the way you think about yourself and your strengths?

_____

_____

_____

_____

_____

_____

One branch of positive psychology has created a "Values in Action Inventory."[10] It's a short online test that allows you to identify what your key character strengths are. We highly recommend you take it.

For each of us, the test was about right. Marina's key strengths are these:

1. Love of learning
2. Creativity
3. Bravery
4. Fairness
5. Social intelligence

These are exactly why Marina is so good at her job. (This is Joan speaking.) Marina's love of learning allows her to pick up knowledge quickly: she has learned her way around social psychology very quickly. Her creativity and bravery means that Joan hired Marina as an administrative assistant, and then she could basically hand over writing large sections of this book. (Yes, her job title changed, too!) Her sense of fairness and social intelligence give her precisely the right combination of world-changing fervor and self-preserving savvy you have seen throughout this book. I'll stop now because I am embarrassing her.

What are your key strengths?

_____

_____

_____

_____

_____

_____

_____

Did you find them surprising or just about what you expected?

_____

_____

_____

_____

_____

_____

How do your key strengths make you a good fit for your dream job?

_____

_____

_____

_____

_____

_____

How are you currently using your key strengths in your current job?

_____

_____

_____

_____

_____

What is one way you could use your key strengths in a new way during the next month (at your job or outside it)?

_____

_____

_____

_____

_____

If you aren't using your key strengths in your current job, that's an important sign. Of course, to get our dream jobs, we may need to do one or more jobs that are less of a good fit. To be able to stretch to do something that doesn't come naturally may be a good thing—especially if there's no way around it!

But if you keep your key strengths in mind, you will be on a good path toward a job you'll be good at and will enjoy. Good luck!

29

Read This When the Unfairness Is Really Getting to You

It gets old. How do you keep your spirits up when you have to keep dealing with this $&#!?

Take a moment to write the things that are getting you down:

_____

_____

_____

_____

_____

_____

Okay, now let's find out what works to pull you out of funks. Joan finds many different tacks helpful, particularly in concert. Marina finds starting one project and diving into it helpful. What works for you?

_____

_____

_____

_____

_____

_____

1. Be Grateful for What You Have

We've said it already: being grateful correlates with happiness. It also helps, when you are irritated at having to deal with gender bias over and over again, to remember to be grateful for all the things that are going *right* for you.

Take a moment to write down four things in your life you are grateful for:

_____

_____

_____

_____

_____

_____

Notice that you don't have to ignore or deny the bad in order to focus on the good things that have come your way.

2. Be Grateful to Those Who Paved the Way

Here's how Joan looks at it: I spent 25 years in a really ugly Tug of War situation, wrote eight law review articles before getting tenure when the requirement was two, spent years being called difficult (or worse) before I learned gender judo, and had a colleague suggest going to a motel together. Granted all that. But here are some things I did *not* have to put with up, unlike the women who came before me: I never was told that I was taking up the seat of a man at law school. I was never fired from a job I loved simply because I was a woman, as my mother was: she was fired from the *Brooklyn Eagle* when the troops came home from World War II. I was never told, as my grandmother was, that I should be ashamed of myself for wanting a career because, as a married woman, my job was to take care of my husband and children.

Here's Marina's take: I spent nine years as a restaurant server, where I was reminded of my gender every day and sometimes made to feel unsafe because of it. I've been asked out by men who I thought were my mentors. I was once told I got a job because I "have a nice smile." As a young and opinionated woman, it sometimes feels hard to be taken seriously. But I've always been able to share my opinions boisterously and never been told to be quiet because I was a woman. I've been able to voice my opinion through other means, like voting and political advocacy, because of women who came before me. And I grew up in a house where my parents encouraged me and my brother equally to pursue careers. Of course, there's much more work to do, but my life would be much, much worse without the women who paved the way.

Spend a few days asking women older than you what it was like in their day. (Careful, some older women survived by repressing it all and won't want to dwell on it. If you meet one like that, just move on.) Just say something like, "I have been thinking how lucky I am to have had people like you pave the way. What was it like when you were my age?" What did you find out? (By the way, this is sometimes a great way to defuse generational conflicts.)

_____

_____

_____

_____

_____

_____

3. Don't Get Mad, Get Even

Okay, we're not saints. Try as we might, we don't go around being grateful all day, every day. Sometimes a little righteous anger is the best fuel there is. *What Works for Women at Work*, for Joan, was partly a process of getting even by trying to ensure that other women did not have to go through, all alone, what she went through. So is the Center for WorkLife Law, which she founded to work toward workplace justice for mothers— and for fathers who play an active role in family life. WorkLife Law now works with companies providing cutting-edge best practice models for interrupting gender and racial bias.

How could you apply the "don't get mad, get even" adage in your own life?

_____

_____

_____

_____

_____

_____

4. Keep In Touch with Righteous Outrage, but Don't Let Anger Take You Over

If you're going to "don't get mad, get even," does that mean that anger has no place? No. Anger is important fuel that keeps the fire of social justice burning.

But don't let it burn you up. Anger is powerful in small doses, carefully aimed to give you energy. But you need to stop long before you're consumed. How do you balance?

One useful approach is to black box it. Use your anger as a way to keep in touch with what you believe is right and to renew your commitment to protest what's just plain wrong. Then take that energy and use it for something positive.

5. Don't Ruminate: If There's No New Thinking There . . .

Reread pages 275–279 of *What Works*, which quotes a truly wise woman who shared something her father taught her. When she was complaining about her job, her dad stopped her, saying that they had gone over that territory before. His advice: either stay because you have decided that there's still something to be learned from staying, or quit if you reach the opposite conclusion: "make a choice to either change it, live with it, manage it, whatever—but make a choice." She wanted to talk through again what was happening to her, but he asked, "Is there any new learning here?" If there isn't, there's no need to discuss it again.

It's a natural human tendency to focus on the negative—that way, you don't get eaten by tigers. There are not many tigers about these days, though. When it comes to ruminating, defined as going over and over and over and over negative things that occurred, just don't. Take the time you need to vent a little and analyze it as needed, but after that, tell yourself that's not allowed. Then distract yourself with something else, preferably something that gives you pleasure (see step 8 below).

Does this sound even remotely feasible? Why or why not?

_____

_____

_____

_____

_____

_____

_____

_____

6. Avoid Anticipatory Regret

Some people interpret "be prepared" as a mandate to anticipate every single thing that could possibly go wrong and think through it in vivid detail. The logic is that if you think it through, then you can be better prepared for it if things go wrong.

Is this something you do?

_____

_____

_____

_____

_____

_____

Did the thing you were so worried about actually happen?

_____

_____

_____

_____

_____

_____

If it didn't happen, well, then it didn't, after you spent all that time and energy worrying about it. If it *did* happen, think of another time when you worried in anticipation about something that never happened:

_____

_____

_____

_____

_____

Joan was brought up to think it was "being realistic" to imagine every grim scenario and adjust to it—just in case it happened. Then one day her husband, Jim, said, "You specialize in anticipatory regret." This comment changed her life. Now her philosophy, within broad limits, is to assume that things will work out, on the theory that if they don't, she will have plenty of time to cope later. The amount of grim thinking she has avoided by abandoning focusing on anticipatory regret is immeasurable.

7. Be Gentle with Yourself

One of the most corrosive things about being in a bad situation is wondering whether, if you had handled things better, you wouldn't be in a bad situation at all.

Don't get us wrong. Sometimes it's helpful to go over a bad situation with someone whose judgment you trust and get feedback. We should all have those kind of people around; if you don't, consult part 3, "Networks."

But once you've done that and made your choice about how to handle the bad situation, don't keep berating yourself about how you wouldn't be in this terrible situation if only you'd handled it better to begin with.

Be gentle with yourself. Joan's daughter, Rachel (and the co-author of *What Works for Women at Work*) told her recently that this is the single most important piece of advice Joan ever gave her. "In my next life, I'll be perfect," Joan always says (though she doesn't believe she could be perfect even if she were given another life!).

You aren't perfect. That's the bad news. Here's the good news: no one else is either. If you are gentle with yourself, you will be less likely to be harsh to others. That's the side benefit. The core benefit is that you can conserve all that energy you otherwise would spend being mean to yourself. And that's a lot of energy.

When was the last time you were harsh with yourself?

_____

_____

_____

_____

_____

_____

Now imagine that your best friend had come to you in exactly that situation, confused and hurt, for advice. Would you have treated her the way you treated yourself? If the answer is no, reimagine how you could have treated yourself with the empathy and understanding you would extend to her and expect her to extend to you.

_____

_____

_____

_____

_____

_____

Do that next time.

8. Remember to Take Pleasure in Everyday Things

As a first step, go back to chapter 28 in the Workbook and do the "Have a Good Day" exercise.

What are the things in your day that give you the most pleasure?

_____

_____

_____

_____

_____

_____

How often do you do them?

_____

_____

_____

_____

_____

If you don't do them every day, which could you do more often? Be realistic. Don't get yourself in a situation where you are stressing out about not being able to do the things that help you destress. But don't hesitate to conclude that because you are going through a hard time right now, you may need to spend more time doing things that give you comfort and energy.

_____

_____

_____

_____

_____

_____

One day recently, Rachel was having a very bad week, and she knew it would be a bad week. So she galvanized into action. One day, after work, she went out and bought a tabloid—she has always been big on tabloids. The next day, she ordered a lipstick online. The third day, she went to yoga. By then, she found she didn't need any more props because she was already more than half over her bad week!

If you are having more than one bad week, then you might also want to reread part 7, "Leave or Stay?," about whether to leave your job or stick it out.

9. Call Out the Bias

Read with "Strategy 4: Address the Bias—With Kid Gloves?" on pages 51–53 of *What Works*.

Prove-It-Again! bias can be painfully obvious, but it's always a professional risk to respond to it. Here are some effective and ineffective responses to common forms of Prove-It-Again! bias that women face.

Situation	Ineffective response	Effective response
In your performance evaluation meeting, your supervisor told you he thought you "need a little more time" to be able to step into a new role—even though your co-worker Tom got promoted with identical metrics.	"You wouldn't be saying that if I were a man."	"I would like to understand how my performance is different from Tom's. Can you help?"
You're in a hiring or promotions meeting, and you realize that your colleagues have found something wrong with all of the female candidates.	"You're being sexist."	"I'm worried we're not evaluating everyone based on the same criteria. Let's define what we're looking for in a candidate and then go back over the pool with that in mind."
Desirable, career-enhancing assignments seem to shower down on Tom, whereas you're stuck with back-office roles.	"I get stuck with the scut work while Tom seems magically to get the good work."	"Can you give me an example of what I would need to do to get the opportunity to do X or Y role?"
You find out your raise is much smaller than that Sam's, whose metrics are similar.	"What do I need to do to get a raise like Sam's? Grow one?"	"Thanks for the feedback on my performance. Can you tell me what I would need to do to get a raise as big as Joe's?"

Situation	Ineffective response	Effective response
Your raise is smaller than you'd hoped, but you don't know how it compares to those of your peers (and you can't ask them).	"I just know I'm being underpaid."	If you can't get information on what other specific individuals are making, ask for the range of what people at your level are making and where you fall in that range. Then ask if anyone with your metrics falls higher in the relevant range.

Conclusion

Enough already. Women have been telling each other that they have to be twice as good to get half as far, that they have to navigate carefully between being seen as a bitch and as a bimbo, that they felt like they a hit a wall when they became mothers, and that they can't believe that women don't support each other more. For years. Decades actually.

We've waited and waited for organizations to fix what's broken. Wait no more.

Implementing *What Works for Women at Work* can help you transition from being frustrated at the same-old, same-oldness of it all and give you new tools to navigate workplaces still shaped by subtle gender bias. Maybe most importantly, implementing these tools when you become a boss can help shape future generations of workplaces for women.

What's the next step for you? As a final exercise, we invite you to write your "Note to Future Self," for when the day comes (and it will come) that you are in a position of power to try and change these patterns. Throughout this book, we have offered you strategies, tips, work-arounds, and other ways to make work more "workable" for you. We hope you are wiser, savvier, and empowered to become your best self. And to that better, happier, more satisfied future self, let us say this: we challenge you when you are the boss to disrupt, change, and eliminate many of the practices and policies of the workplace that women have had to endure for too long.

You don't have to create a workplace utopia (we don't think one exists), but creating a safe space where workers are valued for their best assets, encouraged to flourish, and free to express their most genuine selves feels within reach—a workplace where people like to come to work, maybe not every day or in every moment (again, not gonna happen) but for most days and for most moments. Work will almost always be that thing that you do that allows you to pay the bills, but work can also be that thing that you do where you make friends; push yourself creatively, strategically, and developmentally; establish a career; pursue goals and ambitions; and learn a ton along the way. We hope that we have shown you how to make that happen and that, one day, you pay it forward for someone else, too.

Take a few minutes to write out your "Note to Future Self" and envision a brighter, more empowered future for women and girls everywhere. What will you want to change? What will you leave behind? What will you impress on the next generation?

Note to Future Self

_____

_____

_____

_____

_____

_____

_____

_____

_____

_____

_____

_____

_____

_____

_____

_____

_____

_____

Acknowledgments

Without the wisdom, expertise, and guidance from our colleagues, friends, mentors, and families, this workbook would not have been possible.

Special thanks to Kori Carew, Jean Lee, Jessica Lee, Isabelle Salgado, and Amber Lee Williams for their help in writing part 6, "Talking across Race about Gender Bias." We are inspired by their leadership, resilience, and insight.

Thanks to our agent, Roger Williams of New England Publishing Associates, for his time and energy getting this book off the ground.

Thanks to NYU Press and our editor, Ilene Kalish, for asking us to write the workbook in the first place and then guiding us through the process.

Thanks to Jamie Dolkas, the Center for WorkLife Law's director of women's leadership, for sharing her expertise in networking, using social media, handling difficult conversations, and developing leadership skills.

Thanks to Liz Morris, the Center for WorkLife Law's deputy director, for her patience and understanding while we were frantically writing and rewriting around the office.

Thanks to each and every one of the wonderful staff at WorkLife Law: Liz Morris, Jamie Dolkas, Jessica Lee, Chelsey Crowley, Su Li, Lori Ospina, Lisa McCorkell, Anna Garfink, and Hagar Maimon. Special thanks to Lisa McCorkell for her impeccable attention to detail and generous sharing of her time.

Thanks to the Wise Women and the New Girls—we continue to be inspired by you.

Thanks to Hilary Hardcastle, our library liaison, without whom we literally couldn't write anything.

Thanks to Emily Stover, our research assistant, for her last-minute (and crucial!) fact-checking.

Thanks to everyone at the Center for WorkLife Law and UC Hastings College of the Law.

And, of course, thank you to our families: Joan would like to thank Jim Dempsey, Nick Williams, and Rachel Dempsey. Marina would like to thank her parents and partner for their unfailing patience and support during the best of times ("Oh my god I get to write a book!!") and the worst of times ("Oh my god I'm *never* going to finish this book!!"). She could not have done it without them.

Notes

Introduction

1. Peter Glick, "Trait-Based and Sex-Based Discrimination in Occupational Prestige, Occupational Salary, and Hiring," *Sex Roles* 25, nos. 5–6 (1991): 351–378, doi:10.1007/bf00289761.
2. Ibid.
3. Kieran Snyder, "The Abrasiveness Trap: High-Achieving Men and Women Are Described Differently in Reviews," *Fortune*, August 26, 2014, www.fortune.com.
4. Elizabeth Weisse, "Ellen Pao Begins Testimony in Silicon Valley Sex Bias Trial," *USA Today*, March 9, 2015, www.usatoday.com.
5. Nellie Bowles and Liz Gannes, "Liveblog: As Ellen Pao Takes the Stand, the Test Now Is Likability," *Recode*, March 9, 2015, www.recode.net.
6. Snyder, "Abrasiveness Trap."
7. Shelley J. Correll, Stephen Benard, and In Paik, "Getting a Job: Is There a Motherhood Penalty?," *American Journal of Sociology* 112, no. 5 (2007): 1297–1339, doi:10.1086/511799.
8. "Young Women Top Unpaid Work List," BBC News, February 22, 2008, http://news.bbc.co.uk; Jennifer L. Berdahl and Sue H. Moon, "Workplace Mistreatment of Middle Class Workers Based on Sex, Parenthood, and Caregiving," *Journal of Social Issues* 69, no. 2 (2013): 341–366, doi:10.1111/josi.12018.
9. Joan Williams and Rachel Dempsey, *What Works for Women at Work: Four Patterns Working Women Need to Know* (New York: NYU Press, 2014), xxiii–xxiv.
10. Joan Williams, "Women, Work and the Art of Gender Judo," *Washington Post*, January 24, 2014, www.washingtonpost.com.
11. Christine Yang, "Positive Opinions of Trump Grow after Second Debate, NBC/SurveyMonkey Poll Says," CNBC, October 12, 2016, www.cnbc.com; Jake Miller, "Polls Say Hillary Clinton Won the Debates—Will It Matter?," CBS News, October 20, 2016, www.cbsnews.com.
12. Josh Hafner, "Hillary Clinton's Mid-debate Shimmy Sure Was Something," *USA Today*, September 27, 2016, www.usatoday.com.
13. This list of masculine and feminine traits is taken from the Bem Sex-Role Inventory, the standard test used for assessing perceptions of gender roles. See Cheryl L. Holt and Jon B. Ellis, "Assessing the Current Validity of Bem Sex-Role Inventory," *Sex Roles* 39, nos.11–12 (1998): 929–941.
14. Susan T. Fiske, Jun Xu, and Amy C. Cuddy, "(Dis)respecting versus (Dis)liking: Status and Interdependence Predict Ambivalent Stereotypes of Competence and Warmth," *Journal of Social Issues* 55, no. 3 (1999): 473–489.

Chapter 1. Overcoming Your Own Prove-It-Again! Bias

1. Deborah Tannen, *Talking from 9 to 5: Women and Men at Work* (New York: Quill, 2001), 70.
2. Tara Sophia Mohr, "Why Women Don't Apply for Jobs Unless They're 100% Qualified," *Harvard Business Review*, August 25, 2014, www.hbr.org.

Chapter 2. Overcoming Your Own Tightrope Bias

1. Dana R. Carney, Amy J. C. Cuddy, and Andy J. Yap, "Power Posing: Brief Nonverbal Displays Affect Neuroendocrine Levels and Risk Tolerance," *Psychological Science* 21, no. 10 (2010): 1363–1368, doi:10.1177/0956797610383437.
2. Amy Cuddy, "Your Body Language Shapes Who You Are," Ted Talks, June 2012, www.ted.com.
3. "Jennifer Tilly Dramatically Reads of Bravolebrities' Books," YouTube, October 21, 2013, www.youtube.com/watch?v=ZXUuF0lnVYk.
4. Deborah Gruenfeld, "Power & Influence Discussion Guide," LeanIn.org, March 2013.

5. Joan C. Williams, Katherine W. Phillips, and Erika V. Hall, "Double Jeopardy? Gender Bias against Women in Science," Center for WorkLife Law, UC Hastings College of the Law, 2014, 21, www.worklifelaw.org.

6. Williams and Dempsey, *What Works*, 117.

7. Ibid., 119.

8. Jim Edwards, "Top Female Execs Tell Us Whether It's OK to Burst into Tears at Work," *Business Insider*, April 22, 2013, www.businessinsider.com.

9. Williams and Dempsey, *What Works*, 119.

Chapter 3. Overcoming Your Own Maternal Wall Bias

1. U.S. Bureau of Labor Statistics, "Employment Characteristics of Families Summary," April 22, 2016, www.bls.gov.

2. Anne Weisburg and Ellen Galinsky, "Family Matters: The Business Case for Investing in the Transition to Parenthood," Families and Work Institute, 2014, 12, www.familiesandwork.org.

3. Srini Pillay, "How to Protect Your Employees from Burnout," Fast Company, June 15, 2015, www.fastcompany.com.

4. See Jonathon Lazear, *The Man Who Mistook His Job for a Life: A Chronic Overachiever Finds the Way Home* (New York: Crown, 2001).

5. Diane Kobrynowicz and Monica Biernat, "Decoding Subjective Evaluations: How Stereotypes Provide Shifting Standards," *Journal of Experimental Social Psychology* 33, no. 6 (1997): 579–601, doi:10.1006/jesp.1997.1338.

6. See Daniel S. Shaw and Erin M. Ingoldsby, "Children of Divorce," in *Handbook of Prescriptive Treatments for Children and Adolescents*, 2nd ed., ed. Robert T. Ammerman, Cynthia G. Last, and Michel Hersen (Boston: Allyn and Bacon, 1993), 346–363.

7. See Sharon Meers and Joanna Strober, *Getting to 50/50: How Working Couples Can Have It All by Sharing It All* (New York: Bantam Books, 2013), 17.

8. Ibid., 18.

9. Nancy Gibbs, "Generation Next," *Time*, March 11, 2010.

10. M. S. Granovetter, "Changing Jobs: Channels of Mobility Information in a Suburban Community" (PhD diss., Harvard University, 1970).

11. See Robert O. Blood and Donald M. Wolfe, *Husbands & Wives: The Dynamics of Married Living* (Glencoe, IL: Free Press, 1960).

12. See Meers and Strober, *Getting to 50/50*, 17.

Chapter 4. Avoiding the Tug of War

1. Madeleine K. Albright, keynote speech at "Celebrating Inspiration" luncheon with the WNBA's All-Decade Team, 2006.

2. See Sun Young Lee, Selin Kesebir, Madan M. Pillutla, "Gender Differences in Response to Competition with Same-Gender Coworkers: A Relational Perspective," *Journal of Personality and Social Psychology* 110, no. 6 (2016): 869–886, http://dx.doi.org/10.1037/pspi0000051.

Chapter 6. Make Social Media Work for You

1. Christopher Sibona, "Unfriending on Facebook: Context Collapse and Unfriending Behaviors," *2014 47th Hawaii International Conference on System Sciences*, Waikoloa, HI, 2014, 1676–1685.

2. Amy Campbell, "LinkedIn for Lawyers: Basics, Power Tips and Caveats," Infoworks!, 2010, www.infoworks1.com.

3. Sibona, "Unfriending on Facebook."

Chapter 7. Writing Your Resume and Acing the Interview

1. *Jesperson v. Harrah Operating Company, Inc.*, 444 F.3d 1104, 1108 (9th Cir. 2006).

Chapter 8. Negotiating Starting Salary

1. Linda Babcock and Sara Laschever, *Women Don't Ask: The High Cost of Avoiding Negotiation—and Positive Strategies for Change* (New York: Bantam Books, 2007), 132–133.

2. Ibid., 2.

3. Ibid.

4. Ibid., 7.

5. Hannah Riley Bowles, Linda Babcock, and Lei Lai, "Social Incentives for Gender Differences in the Propensity to Initiate Negotiations: Sometimes It Does Hurt to Ask," *Organizational Behavior and Human Decision Processes* 103, no. 1 (2007): 84–103.

6. Hannah Riley Bowles and Linda Babcock, "How Can Women Escape the Compensation Negotiation Dilemma? Relational Accounts Are One Answer," *Psychology of Women Quarterly* 37, no. 1 (2013): 80–96.

7. Hannah Riley Bowles and Linda Babcock, "Are Outside Offers an Answer to the Compensation Negotiation Dilemma for Women?," *Academy of Management Proceedings*, August 2009, 1–6.

Part III. Networks

1. Ronald S. Burt, *Structural Holes: The Social Structure of Competition* (Cambridge, MA: Harvard University Press, 1995), 187; Joan C. Williams, "The Science of Connecting: Building Value in Business Networks" (unpublished paper, 2016).

2. Ibid.

Chapter 9. Making Connections

1. Ronald S. Burt, *Structural Holes: The Social Structure of Competition* (Cambridge, MA: Harvard University Press, 1995), 187; Williams, "Science of Connecting."

2. Williams, "Science of Connecting."

3. Mark S. Granovetter, *Getting a Job: A Study of Contacts and Careers* (Cambridge, MA: Harvard University Press, 1974).

4. Ibid.

5. Williams, "Science of Connecting."

6. Jung Typology Test, www.humanmetrics.com.

Chapter 11. How Your Work Network Works

1. Rob Cross, Andrew Parker, Laurence Prusak, and Stephen P. Borgatti, "Knowing What We Know: Supporting Knowledge Creation and Sharing in Social Networks," *Organizational Dynamics* 30, no. 2 (2001): 100–120.

2. David Krackhardt and Jeffrey R. Hanson, "Informal Networks: The Company behind the Chart," *Harvard Business Review* 71, no. 4 (1993).

3. Ibid.

4. Williams, "Science of Connecting."

5. Ibid.

Chapter 12. Prove It (Over and Over) Again

1. Williams and Dempsey, *What Works*, 32.

Chapter 13. Are You Doing the Glamour Work or the Office Housework?

1. Tammy D. Allen, "Rewarding Good Citizens: The Relationship between Citizenship Behavior, Gender, and Organizational Rewards," *Journal of Applied Social Psychology* 36 (2006): 120–143.

Chapter 14. Getting Good Performance Evaluations and Getting Promoted

1. Hilary Burns, "Microsoft CEO Tells Women Not to Ask for Raises at the Grace Hopper Conference," Bizjournals.com, October 10, 2014.

2. Deborah M. Kolb, Judith Williams, and Carol Frohlinger, *Her Place at the Table: A Woman's Guide to Negotiating Five Key Challenges to Leadership Success* (San Francisco: Jossey-Bass, 2010), 174.

Chapter 15. Is There a Tug of War On?

1. John D. Sutter, "Marissa Mayer: From Google 'Geek' to Yahoo CEO," CNN.com, July 17, 2012.

2. Susan K. Gardner, "Women Faculty Departures from a Striving Institution: Between a Rock and a Hard Place," *Review of Higher Education* 36, no. 3 (2013): 349–370.

3. Williams and Dempsey, *What Works*, 209.

Chapter 16. Holding Your Own in Meetings and Getting Your Due for Teamwork

1. See Laurie A. Rudman and Julie E. Phelan, "Backlash Effects for Disconfirming Gender Stereotypes in Organizations," *Research in Organizational Behavior* 28 (2008): 61–79.

2. D. H. Zimmermann and C. West, "Sex Roles, Interruptions and Silences in Conversation," *Amsterdam Studies in the Theory and History of Linguistic Science. Series IV, Current Issues in Linguistic Theory* 125 (1996): 211; Cecilia L. Ridgeway, Joseph Berger, and LeRoy Smith, "Nonverbal Cues and Status: An Expectation States Approach," *American Journal of Sociology* 90, no. 5 (1985): 955–978; Faye Crosby and Linda Nyquist, "The Female Register: An Empirical Study of Lakoff's Hypotheses," *Language in Society* 6 (1977): 313–322; Bennett J. Tepper, Sheryl J. Brown, and Marilyn D. Hunt, "Strength of Subordinates' Upward Influence Tactics and Gender Congruency Effects," *Journal of Applied Social Psychology* 23, no. 22 (1993): 1903–1919; Barbara Westbrook Eakins and R. Gene Eakins, *Sex Differences in Human Communication* (Boston: Houghton Mifflin, 1978); Cecilia L. Ridgeway, "Status in Groups: The Importance of Motivation," *American Sociological Review* 47, no. 1 (1982): 76–87.

3. Lynn Smith-Lovin and Charles Brody, "Interruptions in Group Discussions: The Effects of Gender and Group Composition," *American Sociological Review* 54, no. 3 (1989): 424–435; Cecilia L. Ridgeway, "Nonverbal Behavior, Dominance, and the Basis of Status in Task Groups," *American Sociological Review* 52, no. 5 (1987): 683–694; Ridgeway et al., "Nonverbal Cues and Status."

4. Smith-Lovin and Brody, "Interruptions in Group Discussions"; Ridgeway, "Nonverbal Behavior"; Ridgeway et al., "Nonverbal Cues and Status"; Williams and Dempsey, *What Works.*

5. Melissa Thomas-Hunt and Katherine W. Phillips, "When What You Know Is Not Enough: Expertise and Gender Dynamics in Task Groups." *Personality and Social Psychology Bulletin* 30, no. 12 (2004): 1585–1598.

6. M. C. Haynes and M. E. Heilman, "It Had to Be You (Not Me)! Women's Attributional Rationalization of Their Contribution to Successful Joint Work Outcomes," *Personality & Social Psychology Bulletin* 39, no. 7 (2013): 956–969.

7. Karen A. Jehn, "A Multimethod Examination of the Benefits and Detriments of Intragroup Conflict," *Administrative Science Quarterly* 40, no. 2 (1995): 256–282; Karen A. Jehn, "A Qualitative Analysis of Conflict Types and Dimensions in Organizational Groups," *Administrative Science Quarterly* 42, no. 3 (1997): 530–557; Allen C. Amason, "Distinguishing the Effects of Functional and Dysfunctional Conflict on Strategic Decision Making: Resolving a Paradox for Top Management Teams," *Academy of Management Journal* 39, no. 1 (1996): 123–148; Karen A. Jehn, Gregory B. Northcraft, and Margaret A. Neale, "Why Differences Make a Difference: A Field Study of Diversity, Conflict, and Performance in Workgroups," *Administrative Science Quarterly* 44, no. 4 (1999): 741–763.

Chapter 17. Okay, It's Not All in Your Head

1. Correll, Bernard, and Paik, "Getting a Job"; J. Williams, S. Li, and R. Rincon, "Is It the Pipeline, or the Climate, That Leads to a Lack of Diversity in Engineering?" (Center for WorkLife Law, UC Hastings College of the Law & Society of Women Engineers, 2016).

Part V. Handling Difficult Conversations Successfully

1. Douglas Stone, Bruce Patton, and Sheila Heen, *Difficult Conversations: How to Discuss What Matters Most* (New York: Viking, 1999), 7.

Chapter 18. Difficult Conversations at Work

1. Stone, Patton, and Heen, *Difficult Conversations,* 7–8.
2. Ibid., 113.
3. Ibid., 37, 44, 58.
4. Ibid., 171.
5. Ibid., 175.
6. Ibid., 177.
7. Ibid., 181.

Chapter 19. Negotiating Work-Family Conflict

1. Pamela Stone and Meg Lovejoy, "Fast-Track Women and the 'Choice' to Stay Home," *Annals of the American Academy of Political and Social Science* 596, no. 1 (2004): 62–83.

2. Ibid., 76.

3. Faye J. Crosby, Joan C. Williams, and Monica Biernat, "Hitting the Maternal Wall," *Journal of Social Issues* 60, no. 4 (2004): 675–682, doi:10.1111/j.0022–4537.2004.00379.x.

4. Josh Levs, *All In: How Our Work-First Culture Fails Dads, Families, and Businesses—and How We Can Fix It Together* (New York: HarperOne, 2015).

5. Williams and Dempsey, *What Works*, 158.

6. Deborah A. Widiss, "Changing the Marriage Equation," *Washington University Law Review* 89, no. 4 (2012): 721–794.

7. Stephanie Coontz, "The M.R.S. and the Ph.D.," *New York Times*, February 11, 2012, www.nytimes.com.

8. Meers and Strober, *Getting to 50/50*, 46–47.

9. Sarah Damaske, "Changing Rhythms of American Family Life—by Suzanne M. Bianchi, John P. Robinson, & Melissa A. Milkie," *Journal of Marriage and Family* 69, no. 2 (2007): 545–546, doi:10.1111/j.1741–3737.2007.00383.x.

10. Meers and Strober, *Getting to 50/50*, 52; Damaske, "Changing Rhythms."

11. Meers and Strober, *Getting to 50/50*, 46–47, 189.

12. Ibid., 85.

13. Ibid., 197.

14. Ibid.

15. Laurie A. Rudman and Kris Mescher, "Penalizing Men Who Request a Family Leave: Is Flexibility Stigma a Femininity Stigma?," *Journal of Social Issues* 69, no. 2 (2013): 322–340, doi:10.1111/josi.12017.

16. Joan C. Williams, Aaron Platt, and Jessica Lee, "Disruptive Innovation: New Models of Legal Practice," Center for WorkLife Law, University of California Hastings College of the Law, 2015, http://worklifelaw.org.

17. Kerstin Aumann, Ellen Galinsky, and Kenneth Matos, *The New Male Mystique* (National Study of the Changing Workforce, Families and Work Institute, 2011), www.familiesandwork.org.

Part VI. Talking across Race about Gender Bias

1. Williams, Phillips, and Hall, "Double Jeopardy," 6.

2. Ibid., 5.

3. Ibid., 18.

4. Ibid.

5. Ibid., 23.

Chapter 20. Black Women

1. Williams, Phillips, and Hall, "Double Jeopardy," 7.

2. Ibid., 45.

3. Ibid.

4. Ibid.

5. Ibid., 46.

6. Ibid., 45.

7. Ibid., 46.

8. Ibid., 5.

9. Ibid., 6.

10. American Bar Association, Commission on Women in the Profession, *Visible Invisibility: Women of Color in Fortune 500 Legal Departments* (Chicago: American Bar Association, 2012).

11. Williams, Phillips, and Hall, "Double Jeopardy," 6.

12. Ibid., 18.

Chapter 21. Asian American Women

1. Williams, Phillips, and Hall, "Double Jeopardy," 12.

2. Ibid., 16.

3. Dan Nakaso, "Asian Workers Now Dominate Silicon Valley Tech Jobs," *Mercury News*, November 13, 2016, www.mercurynews.com.

4. Williams, Phillips, and Hall, "Double Jeopardy," 12.

5. Ibid., 18.

6. Ibid.

7. Ibid.

8. Ibid.

9. Debra M. Kawahara, Monica S. Pal, and Jean Lau Chin, "The Leadership Experiences of Asian Americans," *Asian American Journal of Psychology* 4, no. 4 (2013): 240–248, doi:10.1037/a0035196.

10. Kolb, Williams, and Frohlinger, *Her Place at the Table*, 174

11. Williams, Phillips, and Hall, "Double Jeopardy," 20.

12. Ibid.

13. Ibid., 28.

14. Ibid., 28–29.

15. Ibid., 29.

Chapter 22. Latina Women

1. Williams, Phillips, and Hall, "Double Jeopardy," 10.

2. Ibid.

3. Ibid., 12.

4. Ibid.

5. Ibid.

6. Ibid., 7.

7. Ibid., 14.

8. Ibid.

9. Ibid., 46.

10. Ibid., 46–47.

11. Ibid., 47.

12. Ibid.

13. Ibid.

14. Ibid.

15. Ibid., 23.

16. Ibid.

17. Ibid., 25.

18. Ibid.

19. Williams and Dempsey, *What Works*, 113.

20. Williams, Phillips, and Hall, "Double Jeopardy," 25–26.

21. Ibid., 25.

22. Ibid., 32.

23. Ibid.

24. Ibid.

25. Ibid.

26. Meers and Strober, *Getting to 50/50*, 28.

27. Williams, Phillips, and Hall, "Double Jeopardy," 31.

28. Ibid., 41.

29. Ibid., 35.

Chapter 23. White Women

1. Williams, Phillips, and Hall, "Double Jeopardy," 5.

2. Joan Williams and Su Li, "Understanding In-House and Law Firm Lawyers' Workplace Experiences," Survey, Center for WorkLife Law, June 22, 2016.

3. Joan C. Williams, Su Li, Roberta Rincon, and Peter Finn, *Climate Control: Gender and Racial Bias in Engineering?* (Center for WorkLife Law, UC Hastings, College of the Law, 2016), http://research.swe.org.

Chapter 24. Sexual Harassment

1. _Robinson v. Jacksonville Shipyards, Inc._, 760 F. Supp. 1486 (M.D. Fla. 1991).
2. Dan Froomkin, "Case Closed: Jones v. Clinton Special Report," _Washington Post_, December 3, 1998, www.washingtonpost.com.
3. Jennifer L. Berdahl, "The Sexual Harassment of Uppity Women," _Journal of Applied Psychology_ 92, no. 2 (2007): 434.
4. Jennifer L. Berdahl and Celia Moore, "Workplace Harassment: Double Jeopardy for Minority Women," _Journal of Applied Psychology_ 91, no. 2 (2006): 426, 432.

Chapter 25. Knowing When to Leave Your Job

1. Karen E. Klein, "How 'Diversity Fatigue' Undermines Business Growth," Bloomberg, May 14, 2012, www.bloomberg.com.
2. Lalith Munasinghe, Tania Reif, and Alice Henriques, "Gender Gap in Wage Returns to Job Tenure and Experience," _Labour Economics_ 15, no. 6 (2008): 1306.
3. Thomas J. Cooke, Paul Boyle, Kenneth Couch, and Peteke Feijten, "A Longitudinal Analysis of Family Migration and the Gender Gap in Earnings in the United States and Great Britain," _Demography_ 46, no. 1 (2009): 147–167.

Chapter 26. How to Leave Your Job without Burning Bridges

1. Williams and Dempsey, _What Works_, 288.

Chapter 27. Work-Life Balance

1. Williams and Dempsey, _What Works_, 201.
2. American Psychological Association, "Exercise Fuels the Brain's Stress Buffers," accessed July 28, 2016, www.apa.org.

Chapter 28. Don't Worry, Be Happy

1. Christopher Peterson, _A Primer in Positive Psychology_ (Oxford: Oxford University Press, 2006).
2. Ibid., 63.
3. Keri J. Brown Kirschman, Rebecca J. Johnson, Jade A. Bender, and Michael C. Roberts, "Positive Psychology for Children and Adolescents: Development, Prevention, and Promotion," in _Oxford Handbook of Positive Psychology_, 2nd ed., ed. Shane J. Lopez and C. R. Snyder (New York: Oxford University Press, 2009), 137.
4. Peterson, _Primer in Positive Psychology_, 127.
5. Angela L. Duckworth, Christopher Peterson, Michael D. Matthews, and Dennis R. Kelly, "Grit: Perseverance and Passion for Long-Term Goals," _Journal of Personality and Social Psychology_ 92, no. 6 (2007): 1087.
6. Peterson, _Primer in Positive Psychology_, 201.
7. Ibid., 38.
8. Ibid., 39.
9. Ibid., 52, 81.
10. VIA Institute on Character, www.viacharacter.org.

Index

About the Authors

Joan C. Williams is Distinguished Professor of Law and Founding Director of the Center for WorkLife Law at the University of California Hastings College of the Law. She is the author of eleven books, including *White Working Class: Overcoming Class Cluelessness in America* and the prize-winning *Unbending Gender: Why Family and Work Conflict and What to Do about It.*

Rachel Dempsey is a writer and attorney. Her writing has appeared in publications including the *Huffington Post* and *Psychology Today*. She lives in Oakland, California, with her partner and two cats.

Marina Multhaup is a Research & Policy Fellow at the Center for WorkLife Law at the University of California, Hastings College of the Law. She attended Oberlin College, where she graduated magna cum laude in politics. She lives in San Francisco with her two cats.